High-Intensity Training

John Philbin

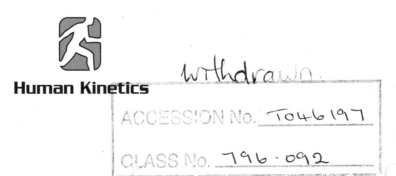

Human Kinetics

Library of Congress Cataloging-in-Publication Data

Philbin, John.
  High intensity training / John Philbin.
    p. cm.
  Includes index.
  ISBN 0-7360-4820-0 (softcover)
  1. Weight training. 2. Bodybuilding. 3. Muscle strength. I. Title.
  GV546.P53 2004
  613.7'13--dc22

2004005760

ISBN: 0-7360-4820-0

Developmental Editor: Susanna Blalock; **Assistant Editor:** Kim Thoren; **Copyeditor:** KLM Words; **Proofreader:** Erin Cler; **Permission Manager:** Toni Harte; **Graphic Designer:** Fred Starbird; **Graphic Artist:** Tara Welsch; **Photo Manager:** Dan Wendt; **Cover Designer:** Keith Blomberg; **Photographer (cover and interior):** Mark Dreibelbis unless otherwise noted; **Art Manager:** Kareema McLendon; **Line Drawings:** Kareema McLendon unless otherwise noted; **Printer:** United Graphics

Human Kinetics books are available at special discounts for bulk purchase. Special editions or book excerpts can also be created to specification. For details, contact the Special Sales Manager at Human Kinetics.

Printed in the United States of America   10 9 8 7 6 5 4 3 2 1

Human Kinetics
Web site: www.HumanKinetics.com

United States: Human Kinetics
P.O. Box 5076
Champaign, IL 61825-5076
800-747-4457
e-mail: humank@hkusa.com

Canada: Human Kinetics
475 Devonshire Road Unit 100
Windsor, ON N8Y 2L5
800-465-7301 (in Canada only)
e-mail: orders@hkcanada.com

Europe: Human Kinetics
107 Bradford Road
Stanningley
Leeds LS28 6AT, United Kingdom
+44 (0) 113 255 5665
e-mail: hk@hkeurope.com

Australia: Human Kinetics
57A Price Avenue
Lower Mitcham, South Australia 5062
08 8277 1555
e-mail: liaw@hkaustralia.com

New Zealand: Human Kinetics
Division of Sports Distributors NZ Ltd.
P.O. Box 300 226 Albany
North Shore City
Auckland
0064 9 448 1207
e-mail: blairc@hknewz.com

Dedicated to my mother, Ann Philbin, and the memory of my father,
Richard M. Philbin (1924-2001).
To my wife, Kazzy; daughter, Bailey; and son, John, Jr.
Thank you for all your patience and support.

Contents

Exercise Finder

Upper Body Push Movements

Exercise	Type	Page
Dumbbell Bench Press	Compound, multijoint, linear	112
Dumbbell Chest Fly	Single joint, isolation, rotary	113
Cable Chest Cross	Single joint, isolation, rotary	114
Dumbbell Decline Press	Compound, multijoint, linear	115
Cable Decline Chest Cross	Single joint, isolation, rotary	116
Dumbbell Incline Press	Compound, multijoint, linear	117
Cable Frontal Raise	Single joint, isolation, rotary	118
Dumbbell Frontal Raise	Single joint, isolation, rotary	119
Cable Incline Chest Cross	Single joint, isolation, rotary	120
Dumbbell Seated Press	Compound, multijoint, linear	121
Machine Lateral Raise	Single joint, isolation, rotary	122
Seated Dip Hammer Press	Compound, multijoint, linear	123
Body Weight Dip	Compound, multijoint, linear	124
Cable Triceps Extension	Single joint, isolation, rotary	125
Cable Kick-Back Triceps Extension	Single joint, isolation, rotary	126

Upper Body Pull Movements

Exercise	Type	Page
Cable Seated Horizontal Row With Lat Emphasis	Compound, multijoint, linear	127
Cable Seated Row With Posterior Deltoid Emphasis	Compound, multijoint, linear	128
Horizontal Pull-ups	Compound, multijoint, linear	129
Prone Iso Post Delt	Single joint, isolation, rotary	130
Dumbbell Iso Post Delt	Single joint, isolation, rotary	131
Cable Decline Seated Low Row	Compound, multijoint, linear	132
Cable Iso Decline Post Delt Fly	Single joint, isolation, rotary	133
Machine Incline High Row Lever	Compound, multijoint, linear	134
Cable Incline Iso High Post Delt	Single joint, isolation, rotary	135
Cable Close Grip Lat Pulldown	Compound, multijoint, linear	136
Cable Wide Grip Lat Pulldown	Compound, multijoint, linear	137
Body Weight Pull-Up	Compound, multijoint, linear	138
Machine Iso Lat Pullover (Super Pullover)	Single joint, isolation, rotary	139
Dumbbell Iso Hammer Curl	Compound, multijoint, linear	140
Cable Iso Biceps Curl	Single joint, isolation, rotary	141

(continued)

Upper Body Pull Movements (continued)

Exercise	Type	Page
Dumbbell Iso Biceps Curl	Single joint, angular	142
Bar Wrist Flexion	Single joint, angular	143
Dumbbell Iso-Lateral Wrist Extension	Single joint, angular	144
Cable Internal Shoulder Rotation	Single joint, isolation, rotary	145
Cable External Shoulder Rotation	Single joint, isolation, rotary	146
Dumbbell Iso Shoulder Shrug	Single joint, isolation, rotary	147
Machine Neck Flexion	Single joint, isolation, rotary	148
Machine Neck Extension	Single joint, isolation, rotary	148
Machine Lateral Neck Left and Right Flexion	Single joint, isolation, rotary	148
Machine Abdominal Crunch	Single joint, isolation, rotary	149

Lower Body Movements: Multijoint and Single Joint

Exercise	Type	Page
Diagonal Body Weight Lower Back Extension	Single joint, isolation, rotary	150
Machine Lower Back Extension	Single joint, isolation, rotary	151
Smith Machine Stiff-Leg Deadlift	Single joint, isolation, rotary	152
Machine Seated Leg Press	Compound, multijoint, linear	153
Machine Sissy Squat	Compound, multijoint, linear	154
Smith Machine Deadlift	Compound, multijoint, linear	155
Dumbbell Lunge	Compound, multijoint, linear	156
Hip Extension	Single joint, isolation, rotary	157
Hip Flexion	Single joint, isolation, rotary	158
Machine Hip Flexion	Single joint, isolation, rotary	159
Machine Hip Abduction	Single joint, isolation, rotary	160
Machine Hip Adduction	Single joint, isolation, rotary	161
Machine Leg Extension	Single joint, isolation, rotary	162
Machine Leg Curl (Flexion)	Single joint, isolation, rotary	163
Seated Machine Leg Curl (Flexion)	Single joint, isolation, rotary	164
Machine Gastrocnemius Raise	Single joint, isolation, rotary	165
Machine Soleus Raise	Single joint, isolation, rotary	166
Manual Shin Curl	Single joint, isolation, rotary	167

Manual Resistance Exercises

Exercise	Type	Page
Prone Decline Push-Up	Multijoint	171
Seated Chest Press	Multijoint	172
Iso Straight Arm Chest Cross	Single joint	173

Exercise	Type	Page
Seated High Row: Post Delt Emphasis	Multijoint	174
Seated Low Row, Close Grip: Lat Emphasis	Multijoint	175
Seated Iso Horizontal Row With Post Delt Emphasis	Multijoint	176
Iso Post Delt	Single joint	177
Iso Prone Post Delt	Single joint	178
Seated Iso Shoulder Press	Multijoint	179
Inverted Seated Shoulder Press	Multijoint	180
Seated Iso Lateral Raise	Single joint	181
Supine Iso Frontal Raise	Single joint	182
Supine Decline Lat Pulldown	Multijoint	183
Supine Iso Lat Pulldown	Single joint	184
Supine Iso Biceps Curl	Single joint	185
Supine Iso Triceps Extension	Single joint	186
Seated Triceps Extension	Single joint	187
Prone Stability Ball Triceps Extension	Single joint	188
Supine Neck Flexion	Single joint	189
Prone Neck Extension	Single joint	190
Seated Neck Lateral Flexion	Single joint	191
Supine Stability Ball Crunch	Single joint	192
Supine Leg Cross Opposite-Elbow-to-Knee Crunch	Single joint	193
Supine Crossover Crunch	Single joint	194
Supine Pure Abs	Single joint	195
Supine Upper Abs	Single joint	196
Supine Oblique Crunch	Single joint	197
Prone Stability Ball Core Abs	Single joint	198
Supine Hip Flexor and Lower Abs	Single joint	199
Prone Stability Ball Decline Hip and Lower Back Extension	Single joint	200
Prone Stability Ball Lower Back Extension	Single joint	201
Prone Stability Ball Decline Iso Hip Extension	Single joint	202
Supine Bench Iso Hip Flexion	Single joint	203
Body Weight Hip and Quad Extension (Sissy Squat)	Multijoint	204
Prone Stability Ball Hamstring Curl	Single joint	205
Iso Hip Abductor	Single joint	206
Iso Hip Adductor	Single joint	207
Standing Iso Lunge	Multijoint	208
Standing Iso Toe Raise	Single joint	209
Seated Iso Shin Curl	Single joint	210

Preface

The high-intensity training (HIT) system embodies a strength training philosophy that focuses on high-intensity work, performing quality repetitions (or reps) to momentary muscular failure (MMF), developing balanced strength throughout each muscle group, and building maximum strength and power in the safest environment possible. The HIT strength system uses the triple progressive overload process, which takes into account not only the number of reps and the amount of weight but also the amount of time the working muscle is exposed to tension. This progressive overload process translates directly into strength gains and facilitates maximum muscle fiber recruitment to ensure the highest level of strength and power development.

The HIT system strives to achieve specific goals during each rep of each set for every workout. Athletes must be mentally prepared to concentrate during each exercise and maintain focus through the entire workout. Every time athletes enter the weight room, the HIT system challenges their willingness to push themselves beyond their current training tolerance for muscle discomfort. Athletes are only as strong as their acquired ability to tolerate muscle discomfort while tapping into the deepest inroads of muscle tissue during the last rep of every set. Most important, thousands of athletes will testify to the fact that the HIT system is by far the most intense but rewarding strength system around. The head strength coach of the Houston Texans, Dan Riley—who has spent 22 years in the NFL—says, "The high-intensity strength system is the most physically and mentally demanding strength system that will take any athlete to the highest level of performance."

The HIT system uses as many strength resistance modalities as possible, including (but not limited to) free weights, machines, cables, and manuals, to facilitate different muscle recruitment patterns. This system can be integrated into any athletic strength training program, regardless of the available equipment, space limitations, or time restrictions—even when there are many athletes in the program.

Athletes from any sport and age can benefit from the HIT system. In addition, physical education teachers, strength coaches, personal and athletic trainers, and rehabilitation specialists will all benefit from reading this book and understanding how the HIT system can be applied.

The HIT system has evolved over the last 30 years since Arthur Jones, the founder of Nautilus, and Dr. Ellington Darden, Nautilus' director of research, published extensive scientific research on its principles and applications. Since 1992 a very highly respected researcher of our time, Dr. Wayne Westcott, has completed hundreds of studies with the HIT system, and he says, "The HIT system is the most effective and practical strength program for all athletes, general population, adolescents, and senior citizens."

   The National Strength Professionals Association (NSPA), which formed in 1985, believes that the HIT strength system is the most effective, most efficient, and safest strength training program available to athletes. In fact, NSPA has documented research and strength records for thousands of athletes over the last 18 years at all levels of sports. This research documents the levels of improvement regarding the building of balanced strength, explosive power, and speed. Consequently, many of the top professional strength coaches across the country believe that the HIT system is, without a doubt, the most time-efficient and effective approach for maximum strength development available for athletes today.

   This book is a compilation of my 25 years of practical experience as a professional strength coach and 18 years as the president of the NSPA. I was introduced to the HIT principles in 1978 as a Nautilus instructor and personal trainer. During the early 1980s, I started my career as an assistant strength coach under one of the most highly respected college strength coaches in the country, Frank Costello, head strength coach at the University of Maryland from 1976 to 1989. I worked directly with athletes in football, basketball, gymnastics, lacrosse, and track and field. In addition, I taught advanced exercise science and strength training to graduate students in kinesiology. In 1982 I did a graduate internship with the Washington Redskins under the legendary HIT guru Dan Riley, who was the head strength coach from 1982 to 2000. Coach Riley and the Redskins won the Super Bowl Championship that year and went on to win two more Super Bowls under head coach Joe Gibbs. From 1993 to 2000 I worked as an assistant strength coach under Coach Riley, who is known for creating numerous opportunities for HIT strength coaches in the NFL. In fact, three generations of HIT strength coaches are in the NFL today serving the dozen teams that use the HIT strength system as the foundation of their in-season and off-season strength program. In addition, numerous Division I collegiate programs, such as those at Penn State, Michigan State, Michigan, Notre Dame, and Toledo, all use the HIT strength system.

   In 1983 I was appointed the head strength coach of the United States Olympic Training Center in Lake Placid, New York. It was here that I started to fine-tune the HIT system for all summer and winter sports with great success. After the 1984 Winter and Summer Olympics, I was fortunate to travel throughout Europe and to the Middle and Far East with the United States Sports Academy, founded by Tom Rosandich, as a strength coach and throwing coach for the country of Bahrain.

   In 1985 I was certified by the National Strength and Conditioning Association (NSCA). It was then that I decided to create the NSPA to promote and teach the HIT strength system. NSPA was recognized in 1999 by the IDEA Health and Fitness Association as one of the nation's leaders in strength and conditioning education and personal training certification. NSPA has certified more than 15,000 strength coaches, physical education teachers, and personal and athletic trainers over the last 18 years; and it continues to grow into the international market. In 1986 I was hired as the director of postrehabilitation and conditioning at the Shady Grove Orthopedic and Sports Medicine Center, where I had amazing results implementing the HIT system. At the same time, I was appointed as the director of strength training for the Achilles track club, which trained hundreds of physically handicapped athletes, many of whom became gold medal winners at the 1988 Para-Olympic Games.

In 1987 I was appointed the director of sports science and conditioning for the United States Olympic bobsled team, and I've been credited for creating some of the fastest push teams in the world during the 1992 Olympics. I was appointed the head coach of the Olympic team for the 1992 Olympics and currently serve on the board of directors. During my coaching tenure with the bobsled team I introduced the HIT system to several world-class sprinters—including Herschel Walker, Edwin Moses, Willie Gault, and Renaldo Nehemiah—with great success. During the 1990s I opened two 20,000-square-foot health clubs (with my partner, Jack Broderick, who has 28 years of HIT experience) called Philbin's Health and Fitness Centers, which grew to serve more than 8,000 members. The success of the clubs was a result of the success members experienced when using the HIT system. In 2000 I sold the clubs to Town Sport International to pursue other ventures.

I've implemented the HIT strength system with thousands of junior high, high school, collegiate, and professional athletes over the last 25 years. I introduced HIT to the professional boxing world and the World Boxing Association between 2000 and 2003. The HIT training philosophies and methodologies helped my world-class athletes win several world championship boxing titles.

The HIT principles, theories, and applications have evolved over three decades to become the fastest-growing strength training system in the 21st century. The HIT system continues to grow in popularity as a result of the continued success of high school, collegiate, and professional athletes that use the program.

The most difficult part of the HIT strength system is learning to create new habits and skills, such as performing the "perfect rep." Some athletes will feel uncomfortable, unsure, and skeptical at first. For the HIT system to be successful, athletes and coaches must implement the contents of this book to perfection. Often athletes will try the HIT system, but will not implement it correctly, so the results will be less than favorable. Once athletes and coaches have successfully mastered the HIT system, however, improvements and increases will occur in the following areas:

▶ Explosive power
▶ Strength and endurance
▶ Speed, quickness, and reaction time
▶ Coordination, agility, balance, and movement efficiency
▶ Lean muscle tissue

- ▸ Flexibility and joint stabilization
- ▸ Tolerance for muscular failure discomfort
- ▸ Anaerobic threshold and basal metabolic rate (BMR)

In addition, decreases will occur in the following areas:

- ▸ Risk of injury in the weight room and on the playing field
- ▸ Lower back and shoulder complications and injuries
- ▸ Recovery time from injuries
- ▸ Body fat
- ▸ Duration of training sessions

In addition to the physical attributes and performance improvement athletes gain by using the HIT system, psychological improvements—such as increased mental toughness, discipline, and confidence—are realized. When implementing the HIT system, athletes will quickly see that it produces results superior to any other strength training program. The HIT methodology is the only system that concentrates on developing balanced maximal strength throughout the entire body, thereby decreasing the risk of injury in the weight room and on the playing field. The HIT system develops explosive power, increases speed, and enhances athletic performance in all sports.

This book focuses specifically on those athletes who are looking to create the most dynamic and effective strength training program available to maximize power and athletic performance. The system has proven to be extremely successful with young athletes, because it does not include any type of ballistic movements that could eventually cause joint injuries. By following the step-by-step protocols in this book, you will learn how to perform the HIT perfect rep to maximize muscle fiber recruitment through the entire strength curve. You will learn just how important each rep and each set is to making maximum gains in the shortest time possible. You will learn how to build a high tolerance for muscular discomfort that will allow you to tap into deeper levels of muscle tissue. This book will also teach you how to develop balanced strength programs and how to use advanced overload training (AOT) to break through strength plateaus. It will enable you to design a year-round strength program that specifically addresses your sport and time restrictions. It will teach you how to perform the "perfect spot" to maximize strength results and will teach you about other performance-enhancing variables outside the weight room, such as nutrition, hydration, and dietary supplements. It will empower you to build maximum strength and explosive power in the shortest time.

The HIT system is the safest and most productive strength program available, but the end result will be determined by your ability to implement the program as it is outlined in this book. Train hard.

Acknowledgments

This book is a product of many highly-respected strength and conditioning coaches, researchers, educators, athletes, and colleagues who must be recognized for their dedication and inspiration to the HIT strength system.

First, I must recognize Jack Broderick, president of FITT, NSPA head instructor, and a contributing author who has 35 years of experience in the health and wellness industry. His knowledge of exercise science, physiology, post-rehabilitation, and nutrition were vital to the successful development of this book. Thanks, Jack.

Thank you Frank Costello, former head strength coach for the University of Maryland, for giving me an opportunity as your assistant, and to Dr. Wayne Westcott of YMCA Research, for your friendship and all you have done for me over the years. And a special thanks to my good friend, Dan Riley, whom I regard as my mentor. You allowed me the opportunity to learn the HIT strength system under your tutelage for 8 years, and I am indebted forever.

I must thank the National Strength Professional Association staff and director Mike Hollandsworth for their support, and a special thank you to Barbara Baldwin and Toby Myles for their invaluable editing skills. Thank you to Brian Case, Mike Kohn, Brad Pratt, Suke Francis, Tim Gearhart, and Jordan Zabrikie for tirelessly demonstrating the exercises for photographer Mark Dreibelbis—thank you, Mark. To Planet Fitness owner Kevin Maselka, and Healthtrax Fitness and LifeBridge Health and Fitness: thank you for opening your doors to us.

Special thanks to the following athletes, friends, and colleagues for their valuable input over the years: Scott Ackerman, Beth Bejeck, Adrian Branch, Ed Archer, Joannie Mallet, Don and Michelle Dillingham, Paul Flaherty, Tim Gearhart, Mike Gibson, Jason Hadeed, JoAnne Hamilton, John Hanrahan, Dr. Brad Hatfield, Mike Hogue, Tre Johnson, Michael Kelly, Dr. Neil King, Mike Kohn, Dr. Ted Lambrinides, Dr. Wayne Leadbetter, Steve Maiorca, Ken Manning, Dave Martin, Sid Miller, Kevin Moody, Steve Murray, Renaldo Nehemiah, Brad Pratt, Rich Snedaker, Allen Stein, Kevin Sweeney, Ed Trainor, James Thrash, David Ungrady, and Doug Werner.

Lastly, a special thank you to Dave Sandler and Ed McNeely for making this book a reality.

Brief History of Strength Training

The history of strength training dates back to the Greek era and includes many humorous stories. Through the sport of bodybuilding and athletic competition, the Romans and Greeks gave us our first exposure to a beautifully defined, well-sculpted body. Think of various artistic depictions of Zeus, Hercules, and Atlas, or more recent sculptures such as Rodin's *The Thinker*. The Greeks and Romans celebrated the human body by competing in the nude, and they relied on genetic potential and primitive training techniques to reach their strength goals. In an era where the strongest were highly regarded in society, those with superior genetics were either athletes or warriors, and the concept of a scientifically based strength training program was not even on the horizon.

During the late 1800s, "strongmen" would travel the country in vaudeville circus acts, performing feats of strength. They would press and squat large animals, such as cows and horses, and heavy objects in all sorts of shapes and sizes. These men did not follow a structured strength training program, nor did they have access to fancy barbell equipment or machines. In fact, they learned the most basic concept of strength training, the overload process, through trial and error. These men were genetically gifted with a large, powerful body type very similar to that of sumo wrestlers in Asian culture.

The strongmen noticed that if they lifted a certain amount of weight for a specific number of reps and then lifted more weight or performed more reps two to three days later, after a period of recovery, they would get bigger and stronger. For some strongmen, this overload process worked well. They often had two to three days of muscle recovery between shows and were rarely injured. Other strongmen, however, had more vigorous schedules and had to display their strength five to six days a week.

Unlike their fellow performers, they found it difficult to progress and stay injury-free because of the lack of time allowed for muscle recovery. But despite these differences, both groups of strongmen did share something in common—they were committed to working hard and pushing their bodies to the limit.

While historical recordings of athleticism and strength are often written as anecdotal observations, there is always evidence showing the use of the fundamental principle of progressive overload. This principle is now referred to as momentary muscular failure (MMF) in the HIT system.

The early 1900s showed significant growth in the strength training field, with the following key occurrences. In the early 1900s, Milo Barbell began marketing barbell equipment and helped create a network for those interested in strength training, resistance equipment, and sharing strength training ideas. Then in 1922 Father Lange put together what most weightlifting historians would consider the first academic weight room at the University of Notre Dame. In 1928 weightlifting competition became an official part of the Olympics with three lifts: press, clean and jerk, and snatch. (Modern Olympic Games only include the latter two lifts.)

By the mid-1940s, research was being conducted to answer questions about the benefits of strength training. During this time, Dr. Thomas Delmore studied the effects of strength training on World War II veterans during their rehabilitation from injury and was instrumental in spearheading the concept of *double progressive overload.* Delmore discovered that the most effective protocol for maximum strength gains was to use three sets of 10 reps, increasing the weight progressively by 25 percent each set. Around the same time, Alvin Roy, who is considered the first personal trainer or strength training consultant, was making his mark by designing resistance training programs for female and male athletes of all levels in a variety of sports.

In the mid-1950s, a man by the name of Jack LaLanne sparked the strength training fitness craze. As the nation's leading personal fitness trainer for the general public, he promoted health and fitness on TV, on the radio, and in books, and he even began a chain of health clubs. LaLanne's focus was on bringing back the more sculpted and toned look for the general population, versus the "strongman" approach, which was achievable for only a few. Today, LaLanne is still showing the world that fitness can always be a part of your life if you train properly and live your life with a healthy attitude. He celebrated his 90th birthday in 2003 and, at that time, was still in incredible shape and functioning as someone half his age.

Competitive bodybuilding also began to take shape during the mid-1950s. Several champions, such as Steve Reeves, Bill Pearl, and Charles Atlas, helped develop the image and popularity of bodybuilding. These men were given credit for bringing the sport of bodybuilding to the forefront in the United States. Joe Weider, who owned five of the top-selling fitness magazines in the country in the year 2000, was the first to take advantage of our nation's growing interest in health and fitness. Weider has built an empire of wealth with fitness-related magazines, supplement products, and strength training equipment.

In the early 1950s York Barbell, which was founded by a successful weightlifting coach named Bob Hoffman, published a magazine by the name of *Strength & Health,* which created a worldwide network promoting the company's equipment and lifts. At the same time, Dr. Richard Berger, MD, began to publish numerous articles on the benefits of strength training. In addition, several universities and professional sports teams hired competitive power lifters and Olympic weightlifters to work with their athletes to increase strength, power, and speed.

During the 1968 Olympics, it became very clear to the world that the East Germans, Bulgarians, and Soviets had an edge in the area of strength and power. Publications such as the *Soviet Sports Review,* edited by Michael Yessis, PhD, were being published. Several strength and fitness magazines also published articles on the Eastern bloc methods of building strength and explosive power through volume system training, Olympic lifts, plyometrics, and supplementation. Today we find that many coaches and athletes still use these strength training techniques and methodologies. Over the last 30 years, however, with scientific research on the relationship between strength training and the response of the musculoskeletal system, the "strength world" has embraced a new strength training approach considered by many strength professionals to be more effective and safer than some of the traditional methodologies and applications.

EVOLUTION OF HIT

In the early 1970s, a man by the name of Arthur Jones started to make his mark on the fitness and strength industry. Jones, along with his director of research, Ellington Darden, PhD, began publishing books and numerous research articles about their new Nautilus strength equipment and one-set theories and principles. By the mid to late 1970s, the new Nautilus equipment and principles had become the most popular training system in the health and fitness industry.

The majority of Olympic and power lifters at the time were not overly impressed with the new Nautilus equipment or with its accompanying HIT principles. The competitive lifting community was not ready to forgo its traditional training methods for new principles and applications. HIT challenged the existing lifting systems and beliefs. The Nautilus approach was not very popular among traditional strength coaches and hard-core free-weight lifters, but it did find a place among the general population.

Jones continued to promote his methods of training and did extensive research with cadets at the United States Military Academy at West Point, where he introduced the HIT system. At the time, Dan Riley was the head

Many Olympic and power lifters were not ready to embrace the new HIT methods and principles when they were first introduced.

strength coach at West Point, and he strongly advocated the use of free weights and traditional high-volume strength training principles. However, being open-minded and always willing to try new and innovative approaches, Riley began to experiment with the Nautilus equipment and principles. He soon discovered that he could obtain substantial results with less time commitment and fewer injuries than with the traditional high-volume lift system. From that time forward, Riley believed that the HIT system was the only way to train athletes safely and effectively for maximal strength gains.

A NEW ERA FOR HIT

Joe Paterno, the head football coach at Penn State, recruited Riley in 1977 to become his head strength coach. This was the beginning of a new era of HIT for strength coaches in the college ranks. Penn State football won the national championship in 1982 and Riley became a hot commodity as one of the top strength coaches in college football.

In 1982, Joe Gibbs, the head football coach for the Washington Redskins, recruited Riley to become his head strength coach. During Riley's first year with the Redskins, he implemented the HIT system in a strength room that consisted of approximately 18 Nautilus pieces. In 1983, after having trained using the HIT strength system, the Washington Redskins won the Super Bowl, and they went on to win several more world championships.

During the mid-1980s, Coach Riley's former assistant at Penn State, Chet Fuhrman, became the head strength coach for the Pittsburgh Steelers. At the same time, Ken Wood, a former employee of Nautilus, became the head strength coach of the Cincinnati Bengals. Coach Riley's first-generation assistants—the Redskins' John Dunn and the Cardinals' Steve Wetzel—continue to influence the growth of HIT by placing their assistant strength coaches with other NFL franchises. There were 12 NFL teams during the 2003 season that used the HIT strength system, and the number of NFL teams implementing the HIT system continues to grow each year.

Arthur Jones sold Nautilus, Inc., in the mid-1980s and created a new company called MedX. This new venture primarily focused on HIT strength training protocols using revolutionary computerized equipment for lower back and cervical rehabilitation. MedX now produces a variety of excellent strength training equipment, giving further validation to the HIT system.

Arthur Jones' son, Gary, started a new line of equipment, called Hammer Strength, in the mid-1980s. Computerized technology was used to design biomechanically correct strength movements based on levers to maximize muscle recruitment through the full range of motion. In addition,

Gary Jones and John Philbin discuss strength training techniques and philosophies.

Ken Hutchins, a former employee of Jones', wrote a book endorsing the "super slow" training philosophy, which is an extension of HIT principles. See chapter 9 for advanced overload training techniques.

In 1985, the National Strength Professionals Association (NSPA) was founded to certify strength coaches and personal trainers with the HIT strength training system. In 1995 Jack Broderick, who had 28 years of HIT experience, joined the NSPA team and helped expand NSPA to become an internationally recognized organization, certifying thousands of strength coaches, physical education teachers, personal trainers, and health care professionals. NSPA has since conducted 18 years of ongoing scientific research on the HIT strength system.

Strength training was around long before there was science to document its benefits, and the simple principle of progressive overload has remained its steady foundation. Strength training philosophies and programs will continue to evolve with better research, equipment, and, most important, trial and error in the trenches; but it's important to remember that the HIT strength system is based on scientific research. Pioneers and researchers such as Arthur Jones, Dr. Ellington Darden, and Dr. Wayne Westcott have validated its effectiveness and seen the method proven by the success of countless athletes across the world for the past 30 years.

2

The HIT Perfect Rep

The foundation of the HIT strength system is performing the perfect repetition. The HIT slow-controlled rep minimizes momentum and maximizes muscle tension and fiber recruitment. This in turn produces optimal strength gains throughout the entire strength curve for the targeted, or primary, muscles performing the lift. It also significantly reduces the risk of musculoskeletal injuries.

The perfect rep is the most important component of any strength training system, but it is often overlooked by athletes and coaches. If 100 high school athletes and coaches were randomly picked from anywhere in the country and asked to describe the perfect rep, they would likely give 100 different descriptions. Most would have very general to no specific guidelines or requirements and would explain that they really never gave it much thought. The point is that most strength programs do not have specific guidelines that describe the difference between a good rep and a bad rep, let alone the perfect rep. In addition, the majority of strength programs tend to focus more on how much weight is lifted, regardless of form and good technique.

The HIT strength training system has been recognized as the only strength system with guidelines for performing the perfect rep, and it clearly defines the difference between a good rep and a bad rep. Anything less than perfect is not accepted, and the rep must be repeated until done correctly. This perfect rep protocol is supported by scientific muscle physiology principles as found in Dr. Wayne Westcott's books and in the fifth edition of Berne and Levy's highly respected exercise science book, *Physiology.* In addition, the NSPA has documented research dating back to 1985 showing hundreds of strength charts from successful Olympic, professional, collegiate, and high school athletes.

Learning how to perform the perfect rep is challenging and takes a great deal of discipline, concentration, and practice; however, the rewards are worth the work. Athletes will develop greater explosive power, balanced strength, and endurance; and they will significantly reduce the risk of injury. Experience shows that athletes who change their lifting style and perform the HIT perfect rep will never go back to previous lifting habits and techniques.

Once athletes master the HIT perfect rep, they will easily recognize the difference between their old technique and the new technique. In fact, when athletes perform the perfect rep, they will experience each rep becoming more difficult and significantly more challenging throughout the full range of motion. The slow, controlled rep will test the athletes' ability to maintain perfect form and not cheat by adding excessive momentum or bouncing the weight. Eventually the athletes will perform sets to momentary muscular failure (MMF) with perfect rep form. Athletes using this method always say they feel a burning sensation deep into the muscle and reach a point neurologically where there is quivering and shaking. This type of physiological response maximizes muscle fiber recruitment and dramatically increases strength. To perform the perfect rep and reach the deepest inroads into the muscle during both the positive and negative phases of the lift, athletes must have the drive and ability to push themselves to a higher level of intensity. *The HIT system is only as effective as the level of intensity that is achieved during each rep.* Effectiveness is also directly related to the athletes' tolerance for muscular discomfort. The old saying "no pain no gain" does hold some truth. By building a higher strength training tolerance for muscle discomfort, athletes facilitate greater muscle fiber recruitment and deeper inroads into fast-twitch recruitment. This discomfort or pain, however, is only appropriate when felt in the muscle, not in the joint.

The HIT system emphasizes the negative phase of the lift, in which the weight is lowered. Greater muscle degradation, or breakdown, can be achieved during the negative phase due to increased muscle friction between the actin and myosin myofibrils. Many strength programs do not emphasize the negative phase of the lift, which is a huge mistake when trying to achieve maximum strength gains. Physiologically, lifters are 40 to 60 percent stronger during the negative phase of the lift and can continue to perform the negative phase even after they can no longer perform the positive phase.

It is common for athletes to experience a learning curve while getting used to performing perfect reps and perfect sets to MMF. In fact, some athletes with years of weightlifting experience will find this transition extremely difficult as they try to break old habits. Sometimes athletes will push themselves to the point of nausea during their first few HIT workouts. This response—the result of muscle and liver glycogen depletion and oxygen debt—is a little different from what the athletes are used to, but it is normal for those learning the HIT system. It is the body's way of responding to a high-intensity anaerobic workload. The body will adapt to this physical stress with positive strength gains, increased explosive power, greater recovery capabilities, and an elevated anaerobic threshold. This physiological adjustment is called general adaptation syndrome (GAS), which is discussed in greater detail in chapter 4.

Eventually the athletes will learn that they are only as strong as the last perfect rep to MMF, and they will appreciate why the HIT strength system requires them to build a higher level of muscular discomfort. This enables them to take their strength training to another level. The HIT system will empower the athletes to reach their peak physical athletic strength potential and help develop mental toughness.

EXECUTING THE PERFECT REP

Prior to executing the HIT perfect rep, athletes must be aware of their own body cues while performing any strength training exercise. They must be able to maintain good orthopedic form, including neutral alignment of the neck, shoulders, lower back, wrists, and pelvis. An example of bad form would be arching the back, extending the neck, and hyperextending the wrists while performing the free-weight bench press. Bad form typically occurs when the weight can no longer be lifted in a controlled manner. This could cause an acute muscle strain or chronic pain to the joint from trauma or soft-tissue damage over time.

To reduce the risk of injury, it is important for athletes to train push and pull muscle groups and stabilizers so that all joints have balanced strength and stabilization. An example of a poor training plan would be to perform multiple sets of the free-weight bench press, working the anterior muscles of the shoulder joint, while neglecting to do an equal number of sets at the same intensity for the seated row, which works the posterior muscles of the shoulder joint. This would create a muscle imbalance, which could lead to serious injury and chronic pain. It is imperative that the selection of exercises and number of sets, as well as intensity of effort, be balanced for all push and pull muscle groups throughout the entire body.

Each exercise should be completed using a full range of motion, without causing negative pain in the joint. It is important for the athlete to be able to know the difference between joint pain and muscle discomfort. An example of negative pain would be a slight twinge of discomfort in the shoulder joint while executing a free-weight bench press or seated shoulder press. Many athletes unfortunately ignore the signs, or red flags, of joint discomfort while performing certain exercises. This is common among dedicated athletes who do not want to stop lifting because they believe that the pain will eventually go away, or athletes who use the readily available over-the-counter nonsteroidal anti-inflammatory drugs to mask the pain. Unfortunately, ignoring the pain could eventually lead to severe rotator cuff or shoulder impingement problems. To remedy the situation, the athlete may need to select an alternative modality or adjust the angle of the bench.

Positive Phase

Establish proper body alignment and begin moving the weight with a slow and controlled positive, concentric contraction. Enlist only the targeted muscle or muscles; do not use additional levers and muscles to control the lift. The goal is to reach the end of the full range of motion within two to three full seconds (figure 2.1). At the end of the positive phase, the targeted muscles must perform a distinct isometric pause—absolutely no bounce or recoil should take place at this point.

When executing multijoint pull movements, focus on increasing the tension at full contraction of the targeted muscles by thinking, *Squeeze and pause,* as the muscles smoothly transition to the negative phase of the rep. When performing multijoint push movements, pause at full contraction while maintaining tension in the targeted muscles. The joints should never lock, because muscle tension would then be released. All single isolation movements must include a distinct pause at full contraction to maximize primary muscle activation. This pause ensures that the athlete has complete control of the weight and that maximum fiber recruitment occurs throughout the full range of motion.

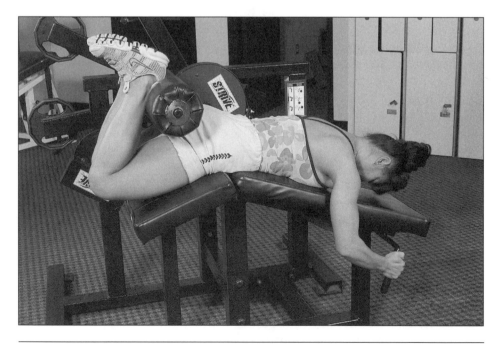

Figure 2.1   The positive (concentric) phase of the lift requires two to three seconds to perform, followed by a distinct isometric pause at full contraction.

Let's use the leg extension as an example of a single isolation movement. When the positive phase is completed—that is, when the leg is at full extension—the weight should not cause the leg to drift backward into the eccentric, or negative, phase . . . not even an eighth of an inch! If an athlete cannot prevent this from occurring, then the weight is too heavy, there was too much momentum during the positive contraction phase, or the athlete may not have focused 100 percent on isometrically squeezing at the top of the full range of motion. Note that the weight stack or weight will always rise during the positive, concentric phase of a lift.

Negative Phase

After the distinct pause at the completion of the positive phase of the lift, begin the controlled descent of the negative contraction of the rep (figure 2.2). The same muscles that raised the weight will lower it. It will take less effort and fewer muscle fibers to lower the weight than it did to raise it. In fact, the negative part of the rep is approximately 40 to 60 percent stronger than the positive phase because of the physiology of the actin/myosin crossbridges creating greater internal muscular friction.

Two ways to increase muscle fiber recruitment during the negative part of the rep are to 1) increase time of tension or 2) add more resistance. For practical reasons it is recommended that athletes slow down the negative phase, which will in turn increase the time of tension. The negative phase

Figure 2.2 The negative (eccentric) phase of the lift requires three to four seconds to perform, followed by a distinct pause at full range prior to the next rep.

should take between three and four full seconds. Note that the weight stack or weight will always be descending during the negative, eccentric phase of a lift.

Rep Transition

During the transition from negative to positive between reps, there should be a controlled and a distinct pause of the weight, while keeping the targeted muscles under constant tension. It is a common mistake not to pause during the transition from negative to positive. Many athletes cheat by bouncing the weight off the body or weight stack while potentially hyperextending or hyperflexing the joint in order to perform what some call a prestretch recoil. This produces unnecessary momentum, which reduces muscle recruitment and can cause soft-tissue damage to the joint.

Transitioning smoothly from negative to positive and from positive to negative will take practice for most athletes to perfect. Keep in mind that push and pull multijoint movement transitions are unique because at the full contraction of a push movement, the joint is extended, while at a full contraction of the pull movement, the joint is flexed. As an athlete begins to fatigue toward the end of a set, the rep transition may dramatically worsen, with a tendency toward increased momentum or a more profound bounce of the weight stack or the athlete's body. Each consecutive rep becomes less controlled, and the athlete must fully concentrate to effectively complete the set. Both positive and negative phases are important for maximum strength; however, it is worth repeating that the negative phase has greater potential to maximize strength gains and cause hypertrophy.

Additional Components of the Perfect Rep

Steady, controlled breathing throughout the entire set is essential for replenishing oxygen, reducing intraocular (eye) pressure, reducing intracranial (brain) pressure, increasing blood flow return to the heart, and controlling blood pressure. Constant oxygen transport to the brain and heart is essential. Recommended breathing methods include exhaling during the positive and inhaling during the negative phase, or constantly breathing with deep even breaths. Breathing in and out during a six-second rep could lead to hyperventilation, so the athlete should always focus on taking meaningful breaths and not shallow, short breaths.

All athletes should use a stopwatch when first learning how to perform the perfect rep. Time the entire set from start to finish. This will enable the athlete to divide the number of reps performed by the total time of tension and then figure out the average rep speed. The goal is to achieve a five- to seven-second average rep speed.

During the perfect rep, the joint should never be compromised at the completion of either the positive or the negative phase. Full range of motion can be achieved without hyperextension, hyperflexion, or an uncontrolled lockout of the joint. If muscle tension is decreased or lost at any point at or near full extension, the athlete should stop short of full range of motion to concentrate on performing an isometric contraction with the primary muscles. In addition, if the perfect rep is performed through the full range of motion, improved flexibility can occur in the targeted muscles.

The perfect rep protocol is used by competitive power lifters across the country. It demonstrates that the athlete is in complete control of the weight and that the targeted muscles are performing the lift without excessive momentum and without bouncing the weight off the stack or body. The perfect rep creates direct accountability and reliability of strength gains. Record only the number of perfect reps completed. Do not count reps that are not HIT perfect reps or that a spotter has assisted during the positive phase of the lift.

QUALITY OF THE REP

The quality of each rep is far more important than the amount of weight being lifted. The HIT rep focuses on the targeted muscles versus a full body lift. The average lifter completes a full rep in approximately one to two seconds. The HIT lifter completes a full rep in five to seven seconds. The time under tension for the HIT lifter is three to six times greater and has cumulatively greater overload through the full range of motion. Following this protocol will lead to balanced strength within the targeted muscles. This cannot be achieved if the rep is performed with excessive momentum, which has the potential to create a muscle imbalance within the targeted muscle.

To gain maximum strength and power from the HIT system, the athlete should never sacrifice perfect form. It is all too common to watch athletes focus on how much weight they can lift using their entire body, with no regard for form or technique. I often cringe when I see people attempt to push too much weight when performing the free-weight bench press—their methods of "cheating" and poor form can easily lead to injury.

The Art of Cheating

The free-weight bench press is by far the most popular upper body strength movement for the male athlete. It is common for some programs to accept any form while benching, as long as the weight makes it back to the starting position. The following is a description of an athlete performing a non-HIT free-weight bench press demonstrating the art of cheating.

The spotter assists the lifter with the weight, placing it over the chest while the lifter's elbows are locked, so that the weight is held by the joints.

Performing HIT perfect reps will enable lifters to reach their genetic strength potential.

The lifter takes one last deep breath and proceeds to unlock the elbows so that the weight then drops toward the chest at approximately the speed of gravity, in less than half a second. Now the lift becomes a contact sport and weight-throwing contest. When the bar bounces off the chest, the lifter simultaneously performs a full body arch and tries to use every ounce of body weight and every possible lever in his body to assist the weight. The athlete improves cheating techniques with each consecutive rep as the weight slows down with muscle fatigue. It is common to see one arm start to drift backward while the other arm desperately tries to stay on track and wrists start to hyperextend. The spotter, seeing all this occurring, moves toward the bar but the lifter angrily says, "Don't touch! I got it!" Fight-or-flight adrenaline kicks in at this point, and the body will twist and turn to do just about anything to get the weight moving in the right direction again. Finally, the spotter assists the lifter and helps carry the weight up to full extension lockout, where the weight is then slammed back into the safety brackets and the loud bang echoes throughout the gym. The athlete then sits up and says, "Did you help me?" The spotter replies, "No way!" The lifter says, "That was easy. I can do more!"

The athlete will consider his last lift a successful one and continue to add more weight to the bar, which means that he will increase his proficiency at cheating. Each set will bring increased momentum, a more profound bounce off the chest, and a higher arching of the back. Consequently, it becomes a question of how much weight the athlete can bounce off the chest while thrusting his back and torso into a high leverage arch. The more the athlete cheats, the greater the possibilities of muscle imbalance and severe injury. The free-weight bench press is considered one of the most effective strength exercises for the chest muscles—if the athlete is performing a perfect rep. However, the anterior deltoids and rotator cuff muscles are under the most stress during this lift. Many athletes experience and ignore signs of shoulder pain and try to work through the discomfort or aggravation, hoping it will disappear. In most cases, the pain increases, leading to a chronic injury such as tendon inflammation and preventing the athlete from continuing the strength program. There are numerous reasons an athlete would experience shoulder pain, such as tendinitis, impingement syndrome, or rotator cuff strain, when performing the free-weight bench press; here are some of those reasons.

First, some athletes were built with favorable biomechanics for performing the free-weight bench press, while others are not so lucky. If an athlete feels any discomfort in the shoulder when performing the free-weight bench press, then he should consider alternative exercise modalities, such as the use of dumbbells or machines. Keep in mind that muscles do not know the difference between free-weight resistance and machine resistance. This holds true for any lift; muscles only know tension.

Second, various injuries can occur to the anterior shoulder musculature and joint when performing one-rep maximums with excessive loads during the bench press. This can happen during the beginning of a strength program when trying to determine the athlete's strength or during preseason when testing with too much weight. Many times the athlete is unable to play an entire season because of injuries caused by inappropriate strength testing methods. The most important rule in any strength program is never to injure an athlete while lifting and, more specifically, not to create an injury potential in the weight room that will be exacerbated on the field of play.

Third, injuries can occur when the athlete bounces the weight off the chest, causing sternum trauma, and thrusts it into the air, using excessive momentum that is ballistic in nature. The elbow and shoulder joints engage to stop the weight's momentum during the positive phase of the lift, which can cause acute or eventual trauma to the joints.

Finally, performing four or more sets of free-weight bench presses, four or more chest exercises with multiple sets, performing too many push exercises, and training the same muscle groups too many times a week can easily lead to overuse injuries. Many athletes spend too much time focusing on their large push muscles and neglect their upper back muscles. This, of course, can also lead to injury and muscle imbalance. Female athletes generally spend less time working with the free-weight bench press and, as a result, do not have these same concerns. In fact, most female athletes, as well as HIT lifters, consider the free-weight bench press no more important than any other lift and do not overemphasize the chest work.

Creating Balance Within a Muscle Group

It is common for athletes and coaches to discuss the general muscle imbalance between push and pull muscle groups, such as the quadriceps versus the hamstrings, but what about muscle balance within the same muscle group? When athletes perform reps at a speed equal to or less than two seconds per rep, they are using too much momentum and are decreasing tension in the working muscle. This also reduces fiber recruitment and will create a muscle imbalance within the targeted muscle.

An example of creating specific muscle imbalance is the way a traditional lifter compares to a HIT lifter when performing the prone leg curl, which is done while lying face down. The traditional reps are often ballistic in nature and look more like a butterfly stroke than a prone leg curl. Of course, as the set progresses, the reps get continually worse and the muscle balance within the targeted muscles—in this case, the hamstrings—declines. See table 2.1 for the difference between HIT and traditional lifts.

This type of ballistic leg curl is the cause of significant strength imbalance within the hamstring muscles and dramatically increases the risk

Table 2.1 HIT Lifts Versus Traditional Lifts

HIT	Traditional
The athlete keeps the back in a natural position and rests the chest on the machine while slowly beginning a controlled rep.	The athlete hyperextends the back and swings the upper torso down to initiate the movement of lifting the weight off the stack.
The weight is controlled throughout the positive full range of motion and takes 3 sec. to complete.	The weight is then accelerated through the positive three-quarters of the range of motion in about 1 sec.
At the end of the full contraction of the positive phase, there is a distinct .5-sec. pause and squeeze that elicits maximum fiber recruitment at the top end of the strength curl.	The hips rise off the bench into a high lower back arch as the resistance swings immediately back into the negative.
After the pause at the top of the positive phase, the controlled negative phase begins and will take 4 sec. to complete.	The resistance is then lowered in an uncontrolled negative phase while accelerating back to the starting position in less than 1 sec.
At the end of the negative phase there is a slight pause to show full range of motion and control. The muscle tension should never leave the hamstrings, and then the next controlled rep will begin.	At the end of the negative phase, there is a simultaneous weight stack bounce and hyperextension of the back to initiate the recoil of the weight into the next rep.

of hamstring pulls, strains, and lower back trauma. Moreover, it also creates imbalance with the antagonistic muscles of the thigh and hip flexors. Besides not allowing maximum muscle fiber recruitment, this improper rep will never produce muscle nerve activation in the last 15 to 20 degrees of the range of motion. This can cause hamstring limitations during sprinting or a similar athletic movement. Hamstring and other muscular limitations should never be a limiting factor with a well-conditioned athlete and can be fixed if the proper rep is implemented. NSPA has documented research of hundreds of athletes switching from traditional strength training methods with bad form to the HIT system over the past 18 years. The majority of these athletes have had significant imbalances in strength curves and specifically in the range of motion and strength curve for their hamstrings. After using the HIT system, these athletes dramatically improved strength balance with significantly fewer hamstring injuries.

DETERMINING FULL RANGE OF MOTION

To maximize muscular performance, each athlete must first identify his or her full range of motion by performing the movement with light weight. Once the range of motion is determined, the athlete should perform a set of 10 perfect reps using a weight that is about half of what he or she would normally use for that exercise. As more weight is added, the athlete must complete each leg curl to the same spot that was reached when performing the exercise with the light weight. Most athletes have experienced muscle cramps in their hamstrings because they have never recruited muscle fibers at full knee flexion. When using the HIT system, begin with a lighter weight and focus on creating the perfect rep until a complete set of 12 reps can be performed through the full strength curve without cramping or cheating. Once this is accomplished, the overload process begins. Keep in mind that good flexibility will enhance overall strength and power. It is not unusual for athletes to feel extremely sore from delayed onset of muscle soreness (DOMS) two to three days after performing one set of perfect reps without reaching MMF. Most athletes are amazed at the lack of strength throughout the full range of motion, especially at the upper half of the leg curl. It is a humbling and eye-opening experience.

When learning the HIT system, athletes need to reeducate their muscles to prepare them for continuous tension and maximum recruitment of fibers throughout the entire strength curve. Performing the HIT perfect rep can be difficult and very challenging because of old habits that have been ingrained for many years. It was enjoyable to watch the NFL rookies' first day in the Washington Redskins' weight room. These young, genetically gifted athletes came from some of the top college strength programs across the country. The strength coaches would demonstrate to them how reps would need to be done in this weight room. They all looked puzzled and confused. Of course, the veterans—who had experienced the same reaction when they started—were laughing in the background. In one instance, the All-Pro lineman Tre Johnson passed by with confidence and said, "Pay attention, fellas, and listen, because it is going to get ugly when you start with the full-blown HIT workout. It is an education, and you're going to hate it . . . but love the results—I guarantee it!"

Genetics and Muscle Physiology

I t is very clear at a young age that some athletes are born with genetic gifts—thanks to Mom and Dad—that allow them to jump higher and run faster than other kids. Young athletes typically gravitate toward sports and positions that favor their body type, which in turn make them feel more comfortable and successful. These sports and the specific positions within each sport generally favor their body type, height, and genetic attributes. Parents and coaches also tend to choose the sport and position a child will play based on the child's body type and psychological profile.

The HIT strength system is ideal for any young athlete who is trying to improve speed, power, endurance, and overall athleticism—regardless of body type—because it helps to create safe and sound lifting habits that prevent overuse injuries in all sports. Children as young as 10 can begin to perform resistance training under the strict guidance of a certified HIT specialist. Elite gymnasts as young as 8 years old have used the HIT principles under the watchful eyes of coaches.

This chapter explores genetic factors that affect training outcomes, as well as other variables that influence maximum strength gains despite genetic predisposition. Following is a breakdown of different body types, better known as *somatotypes.* This is a commonly used method of classifying body structure into three basic body types according to generalized characteristics, such as body shape and bone size.

Endomorph

- ▸ Small bone diameter at the wrist and ankle
- ▸ Spherical, apple, or pear shape
- ▸ High body weight

▶ High percentage of body fat

▶ Low percentage of muscle mass

▶ High percentage of slow-twitch muscle fibers

Mesomorph

▶ Large bone diameter at the wrist and ankle

▶ Square or rectangular shape with prominent muscularity and wide shoulders

▶ Moderate to high body weight

▶ Middle to low percentage of body fat

▶ High percentage of muscle mass

▶ High percentage of fast-twitch fibers

Ectomorph

▶ Small bone diameter at the wrist and ankle

▶ Angular body shape with narrow hips and shoulders

▶ Low body weight

▶ Low percentage of body fat

▶ Low percentage of muscle mass

▶ High percentage of slow-twitch fibers

A person's somatotype is genetically predetermined and not likely to change with age, diet, or physical training. For instance, endomorphs that follow a strict diet and run long distances may become leaner, but they are still considered endomorphs because of such characteristics as small bone size, high percentage of slow-twitch muscle fibers, and high percentage of body fat. Similarly, if an ectomorph were to strength-train and consume a high-calorie diet in an effort to look like a mesomorph, that person would get stronger, but hypertrophy would not occur to the same extent that it would with a mesomorph. Additionally, the small bones and narrow shoulders associated with the ectomorph would still be apparent. Most athletes are a combination of two somatotypes. See table 3.1 for examples of average professional or Olympic athlete body types.

Because strength gains can be affected by genetics, athletes should focus on their individual goals and not compare themselves to other athletes' progress or strength levels. However, if comparisons of strength levels are needed, the following pound-for-pound strength formula can be used by performing a set to MMF with perfect reps ranging from four to eight reps. Do not allow maximum strength testing using three or fewer reps; the weight required for achieving MMF at such few reps could cause injury.

An ectomorph has characteristics like low body weight, small bone diameter, and high percentage of slow-twitch fibers.

Once you've determined how many reps it takes to reach MMF, find the estimated percentage of one rep maximum (RM) in table 3.2 and use this formula:

Amount of weight lifted ÷ percentage of 1RM = estimated 1RM
estimated 1RM ÷ athlete's weight = strength ratio

For example:

Athlete A weighs 150 pounds and performs 6 reps of the bench press with 170 pounds.

170 ÷ .85 = 200 (estimated 1RM)
200 ÷ 150 = 1.33 (strength ratio)

Athlete B weighs 220 pounds and performs 6 reps of the bench press with 225 pounds.

225 ÷ .85 = 265 (estimated 1RM)
265 ÷ 220 = 1.20 (strength ratio)

Table 3.1 Athlete Body Types and Characteristics

Athlete	Body type	Weight	Body fat	Height	Other traits
NFL lineman or Olympic shot-putter	Large mesomorph	285-325 lbs.	16-22%	6' 2"-6' 8"	Superior muscle strength and hypertrophy, explosive power, quick reaction time, low endurance
Olympic female gymnast or ice skater	Ectomorph/ mesomorph	90-115 lbs.	8-10%	4'8"-5'2"	Superior flexibility and balance, high strength-and-power-to-size ratio, low endurance
Professional basketball player (female)	Ectomorph/ mesomorph	140-175 lbs.	12-16%	5'8"-6'2"	Predominantly fast-twitch fibers (glycolytic type II), explosive power, high anaerobic threshold
Professional basketball player (male)	Ectomorph/ mesomorph and mesomorph/ endomorph	200-240 lbs.	6-12%	6'4"-6'9"	
World-class triathlete or marathoner (female)	Ectomorph	105-125 lbs.	7-11%	5'2"-5'6"	Superior aerobic endurance and predominantly slow-twitch fibers (oxidative type I)
World-class triathlete or marathoner (male)	Ectomorph	140-160 lbs.	4-8%	5'5"-5'9"	

Table 3.2 Estimated Percentage of 1RM

Number of reps	Maximum percentage
4 reps	90%
5 reps	87.5%
6 reps	85%
7 reps	82.5%
8 reps	80%

Regardless of body type and height, some athletes have the ability to develop greater strength and size because of predetermined genetic strength factors. Those predetermined factors include gender, superior muscle recruitment, muscle fiber efficiency, fast- and slow-twitch muscle fiber ratio, muscle length, limb length, and muscle insertion point.

Males in general have greater muscle mass and higher levels of testosterone than females, which allows them the opportunity to develop larger and stronger muscles. However, females are just as strong when comparing their lean body weight strength to that of their male counterparts. Females also increase relative strength at the same rate as males. There will always be a small percentage of both males and females who are exceptions to the rule. They typically have a higher-than-normal amount of testosterone, which allows them to get stronger and bigger than others with the same body type.

Superior muscle recruitment exists when an average amount of muscle mass is linked with a high level of neuromuscular efficiency. An athlete with superior recruitment is able to do more physical work than one who has an average amount of muscle mass linked to a relatively low level of neuromuscular efficiency. Similarly, muscle fiber efficiency is the ability of the neuromuscular system to use fewer motor units to accomplish the same amount of work. Exceptional motor efficiency is due to superior neuromuscular physiology. Neuromuscular efficiency as it specifically relates to the type of sport or activity is an undisputed element of athletic success.

Fast- and slow-twitch muscle fiber ratio is critical in determining an athlete's success at different sports. With all else being equal, an athlete who has a significantly higher percentage of fast-twitch fibers, known as type II, glycolytic fibers, will have a greater ability to develop strength and power. On the other hand, an athlete who has a significantly higher percentage of slow-twitch fibers, known as type I, oxidative fibers, will have a greater ability to develop muscle endurance and stamina. Fast- and slow-twitch muscles will be discussed later in this chapter.

The extent to which a muscle can develop in size and strength is limited by its fiber type, muscle belly cross-sectional area, and overall length. With all other factors being equal, a person with relatively longer muscles and shorter tendons has a greater potential for muscle growth and strength than a person with shorter muscles and longer tendons. This applies to all skeletal muscles of the body. The body's anatomical lever system is also a dominant factor affecting muscle power and strength. A person's limb length significantly alters the angles of force and the potential for force output. A working muscle attached to relatively short limbs can lift more weight than it would under the same conditions attached to longer limbs because of mechanical advantage. Muscle origins are generally located at the same place for all humans and thus have little effect on mechanical leverage; however, the point of insertion may differ slightly from person to person. This is significant because the farther away from the joint a muscle tendon inserts (even by as little as 1 millimeter), the greater its mechanical advantage, assuming that the bone length is the same.

Most athletes have a combination of favorable strength attributes, but it is rare to find an athlete who is blessed with every genetic strength factor. For example, I have had the privilege of working with hundreds of athletes who typify the genetically gifted athlete. The truly genetically gifted strength athlete is usually dominant in explosive sports at a young age and eventually performs exceptionally well in high school and college. On the other hand, athletes who don't exhibit strength attributes at an early age often gravitate toward aerobic, endurance-based sports and perform exceptionally well. Because the HIT system can help maximize muscle endurance and stamina, it can be very useful in assisting all these athletes in developing their athletic potential.

NEUROMUSCULAR INHIBITORS

An athlete who begins a strength training program will see significant gains in the first few weeks, primarily because of a neurological learning curve and improved neuromuscular coordination. The central nervous system (CNS) will learn how to become more efficient with each exercise, reducing the number of neuromuscular inhibitors that impede muscle recruitment. At the end of the full range of motion, both positive and negative, the CNS will activate neuromuscular inhibitors that provide protection to the muscles, tendons, and ligaments from excessive forces and soft-tissue damage. These inhibitors, also called sensory receptors or proprioceptors, are protective reflexes that reduce or inhibit the intensity of muscle contraction and prevent excessive stretch. The two primary types of proprioceptors are the Golgi tendon organs and muscle spindles.

If the athlete performs the HIT perfect rep and controls the weight with minimum momentum at the end of the full range, the sensory receptors that protect the tendon from excessive forces are less likely to activate. On the other hand, a rep performed with greater momentum and less control of the weight at the end of full range of motion causes greater activation of proprioceptors to protect the tendon from injury. The athlete's goal is to maximize fiber recruitment to improve strength and enhance power. Since bouncing, jerking, or recoiling weight will only trigger the natural protective devices, the athlete should strive to lift with smooth and controlled movements.

Most athletes are unaware of these protective mechanisms and as a result do not reach their genetic athletic strength potential. Instead, they develop an imbalanced strength curve within the muscle. This then creates a chain reaction of deficient links that manifests into muscle imbalance between push and pull muscle groups. The solution for this problem is to perform the perfect rep to create balance within the specific muscles. It is also important to develop a balanced program that will emphasize equal push and pull exercises and not overemphasize specific push muscles by focusing on such lifts as the bench, incline, and decline press; dips; and push-ups. More details on programming are included in chapter 7.

One of the protective sensory receptors, the Golgi tendon organ (GTO), which is located in the tendon, senses the degree of muscle tension by monitoring tendon length. When the GTO senses excessive momentum or force, it inhibits further muscle contraction by reducing motor unit recruitment and muscle firing. This is why it's best to minimize momentum during the perfect rep, especially at full flexion and extension. The goal is to produce maximum strength throughout the entire range of motion so that explosive power and peak performance is increased during athletic endeavors.

The other protective reflex mechanism is the muscle spindle (MS), which is located in the muscle and is parallel to the working muscle fibers. It is a specialized group of nerve fibers that monitors excessive degrees or rates of stretch within the muscle and causes the muscle to contract when such a stretch is experienced. These fibers, also known as intrafusal fibers, are separated from the ordinary, extrafusal fibers by a layer of connective tissue. These sensory receptors monitor the extent or rate of stretch within the extrafusal muscle fibers; initiate a rapid, reflex response to overstretching by causing extrafusal fiber contraction; and reestablish proper spindle length through contraction of intrafusal fibers.

MUSCLE FIBER CHARACTERISTICS

The two major categories of muscle fibers are slow-twitch, also known as type I, and fast-twitch, also known as type II. Fiber types are distinguished from each other according to speed of contraction, level of force production, rate of fatigue, and source of energy—oxygen, a combination of oxygen and glycogen, or glycogen (see table 3.3).

Slow-twitch muscle fibers have slower shortening speeds and help perform activities requiring aerobic, or oxidative, metabolism of energy. They contain smaller motor units than fast-twitch muscle fibers, larger mitochondria (the organelles used to convert food nutrients into energy) and related enzymes, and more blood capillaries and intercellular fat. Slow-twitch fibers are more resistant to fatigue than fast-twitch fibers. They are able to produce low-force contractions for a relatively long period. Slow-twitch muscle fibers are high in myoglobin, a red-pigmented protein involved in oxygen transport and utilization, and are therefore darker red in color than fast-twitch fibers. Elite long-distance aerobic athletes, such as marathoners, have been shown to have a significantly greater amount of slow-twitch muscle fibers than most other people.

Table 3.3   Types of Muscle Fiber

Characteristic	Slow-twitch (type I)	Fast-twitch (type II)
Color	Red	White
Fiber size	Smaller	Larger
Recruitment order	First	Last
Activation Threshold	Low	High
Potential for increasing muscle size	Low	High
Fiber makeup	More mitochondria, more endurance enzymes, densely surrounded by blood capillaries; more intracellular fat; more intramuscular triglyceride stores; high concentration of myoglobin, glycogen, triglycerides	More contractile proteins, more glycolytic enzymes, more intramuscular phosphate stores, more myosin ATPase activity, more enzymes for anaerobic breakdown of glycogen and glucose
Aerobic/oxidative capacity	High	Low
Anaerobic/glycolytic capacity	Low	High
Innervation	Innervated by smaller motor neurons, which respond slowly to stimulation	Innervated by large motor neurons that have higher activation thresholds
Force production	Low, over a long period of time	High, over a short period of time
Sports suited for	Aerobic activities (i.e., distance running, cycling, swimming)	Anaerobic activities (i.e., sprinting, throwing, competitive weightlifting)
Exercise level	Low intensity	High intensity

Fast-twitch muscle fibers have faster shortening speeds than slow-twitch fibers and are used to perform muscle contractions with maximal force for explosive movements. They produce greater myosin adenosine triphosphate (ATP) activity, the process by which ATP is broken down to release energy to enable muscle contraction. Fast-twitch fibers typically comprise larger motor units than slow-twitch fibers and are able to produce high force contractions for relatively short periods. They are low in myoglobin and, therefore, more white in color. World-class sprinters have been shown to have a significantly greater amount of fast-twitch muscle fibers than most other people.

The current research has broken down type II fibers into six subcategories, but for the purpose of simplicity, this text will use two categories: type IIa and type IIb. Type IIa is considered an intermediate muscle fiber that shares both type I characteristics and type II characteristics. According to research, type IIa fibers improve the oxidative capacity of fast-twitch fibers if the training stimulus is primarily aerobic. The opposite is true if the training stimulus is predominately anaerobic—that is, without oxygen. The fibers then take on more glycolytic, or nonaerobic, characteristics. It is theorized that type IIa fibers do not change contractile speed but that their metabolic characteristics do change according to the type of training stimulus. For instance, if an athlete participates in a sport that is purely anaerobic in nature, such as football or volleyball, then it does not make sense to train the intermediate fibers aerobically with distance running. These fibers need to be trained anaerobically with sprints and weightlifting so that they can take on those fast-twitch glycolytic characteristics needed for the activity.

MUSCLE FIBER RECRUITMENT PATTERNS

Because fast-twitch muscle fibers are responsible for maximum strength and power, some athletes believe that the faster they move the weight, the greater the number of fast-twitch fibers of types IIa and IIb will be recruited. Many athletes also believe that moving the weight faster while lifting weights will enhance explosive power on the playing field. This theory could not be further from the truth.

Athletes must keep in mind that maximum tension on the muscle throughout the full movement range will recruit the greatest number of type IIa and IIb fast-twitch muscle fibers. This theory is backed by the size principle of recruitment, which states that selection of muscle fibers and nerves follows an order of efficiency, such as smallest to largest. In general, muscle fiber groups containing smaller slow-twitch, type I muscle fibers are activated first, followed by increasingly larger muscle fiber groups of fast-twitch fibers, depending on the amount of tension. In other words, the greater the muscle tension experienced by the targeted muscles, the greater the number of type IIa and IIb fast-twitch fibers recruited.

Thus, the type I fibers will be recruited before the type II fibers, and the CNS will only recruit the specific number of fibers necessary to do the work—no more and no less. Case in point: If the resistance on a muscle changes during a rep, the CNS will immediately adjust accordingly. If the resistance or tension increases, a greater number of fibers are recruited, smallest to largest, to perform the work. Likewise, if the resistance decreases, then the CNS will deactivate fibers in reverse order, from fast-twitch to slow-twitch, to decrease the amount of tension necessary to perform the work.

Athletes looking for maximum strength gains must understand the theory of fiber recruitment order and must control the weight at all times during the perfect rep to maintain recruitment of fast-twitch fibers. Otherwise, increased momentum during the rep will decrease the number of fast-twitch muscle fibers recruited during the contraction, and negatively affect the potential for maximum strength and power output.

Figure 3.1 illustrates a subject performing maximum efforts on an isokinetic leg extension machine at different speeds. It is clear that the greatest muscle tension and force are produced at the lower speeds, such as at 60 degrees per second. As the speed of movement increases to 120 degrees per second, the amount of tension, or muscle force, decreases.

SKILL-SPECIFIC NEUROLOGICAL SPECIFICITY

It is not uncommon to see athletes trying to mimic sport-specific movements and skills in the weight room by setting up activities using cables, dumbbells, medicine balls, and bungee cords in hopes that they'll enhance their baseball throwing, tennis swing, or golf swing. HIT advocates and many motor learning experts suggest that these types of activities are

Figure 3.1 Muscle force and tension decrease as exercise speed increases. The HIT rep minimizes momentum in order to maximize muscle force and tension.

not beneficial for sport-specific neurological movement patterns and may override the fine motor skills and potentially create overuse tendinitis symptoms or acute strains. Instead, sport-specific movements should be performed outside the weight room so that the exact specificity of each skill can be reinforced through practice and repetition.

This type of motor learning and skill acquisition depends on many variables, which require that the elements used in training match the elements found in the athletic contest. The first variable, *muscle specificity,* refers to using the same muscle in the exercise or drill that is used to perform the athletic skill. The movement pattern used in the exercise must also be exactly the same as that used in the athletic skill; this is called *movement specificity. Speed specificity* requires that the speed of movement used in the exercise match the speed used in the athletic skill. Similarly, *neurological specificity* means that the motor neuron recruitment pattern should be identical to that of the specific movement pattern, and *resistance specificity* requires that the exercise resistance must be identical to the external resistance encountered in the athletic skill. HIT practitioners agree with the motor learning experts who believe that, to enhance the skill, all components of the skill practice must be identical to those of the skill throughout the entire range of motion.

The goal of the HIT program is to increase strength for all the muscle groups that directly affect effort during sport-specific movement patterns. Trying to imitate a sport-specific movement skill in the weight room will create negative transfer of sensitive neurological pathways. If a skill (such as javelin or golf) requires an implement, then that specific implement should be used to perfect the neurological pathways for that particular skill. If the implement is released during the sport, then the implement should be released while practicing the skill—the skill should not be practiced with a weight or implement that is never released from the hand, which could cause joint trauma. Additionally, weights or implements used in training should not be significantly lighter or heavier than what is used during sport performance. Doing so could interfere with perfecting neurological specificity.

Athletes should avoid targeting specific muscle groups in the weight room, because this can lead to muscle imbalances, weak links, and eventual injury. Instead, athletes should focus on a well-rounded strength program that emphasizes balance and foundational strength for all muscle groups. This will create a strong structural foundation for enhancing sport-specific skills which should be done on the playing field.

Core training and stability ball skills are very popular among today's fitness trainers and athletes. These types of skills require athletes to balance on balls, discs, or balance boards while simultaneously performing some form of resistance training. Many of these movements are neurologically skill specific and place high demands on core, stabilizing, and postural muscles for balance. These types of neurologically challenging exercises have their place, such as in rehabilitation after an injury, but athletes should not lose sight of building a strong foundation of strength throughout all major muscle groups. In fact, substituting an exercise can be a good way to challenge an athlete. For example, I sometimes have athletes perform the chest press with stability ball push-ups. I apply manual resistance while the athletes perform a set of push-ups with their feet on the stability ball and their hands on the Smith machine bar. The goal is to reach MMF within the desired rep range, which will uniquely challenge not only the primary muscles but also the core muscles supporting the push-up.

This chapter provides a foundation of muscle physiology and exercise science that explains the benefits of performing perfect reps. In my experience, I have found that HIT athletes strive to educate themselves and make it a point to understand everything there is to know about the HIT system. In fact, I find that they often become ambassadors for the HIT program and take it upon themselves to help other athletes learn the system. In essence, they become part of the "HIT family."

Triple Progressive Overload Process

The overload process is the most fundamental principle of strength training. To achieve maximum strength from the HIT system, athletes must fully understand how to implement the triple progressive overload process. As this chapter explains, the overload process not only adds weight or reps but also addresses the time under tension. The intensity of effort dictates the level of muscle tissue breakdown and determines the recovery time necessary for optimum muscle repair and growth. This chapter also discusses the number of sets that are necessary, the best rep ranges for different sports, and the symptoms of overtraining.

The overload process is the most effective technique for breaking down muscle fibers, an event known as microtrauma. In the overload process, the amount of applied stress is increased until it reaches a point of overload. It's important to keep in mind that the muscles get weaker during each resistance training session as they are being microscopically damaged; it is only during the recovery period that they become stronger. Following the appropriate overload, there must be an appropriate period of recovery for the muscle tissue to completely heal and repair itself. This recovery is known as supercompensation. If an athlete allows an adequate to optimal amount of time for recovery and takes in proper nourishment, the "damaged" muscle tissue will respond by getting stronger and larger. This is called the adaptation principle or, more explicitly, the *specific adaptation to imposed demand* (SAID) principle.

If the athlete does not stimulate the muscle with an overload that is greater than that of the previous workout, the muscle will not respond with increased strength because it is not being pushed beyond its present level of strength. If, however, the athlete stimulates the muscle tissue with a greater overload than in the previous workout, the muscle tissue will respond with increased strength. It is important to keep in mind that once athletes reach their peak athletic strength during the off-season, they must maintain that same level of intensity and overload throughout the season or they will lose a significant amount of strength.

TRIPLE PROGRESSIVE OVERLOAD

The *double progressive* overload technique involves adding weight and increasing the number of reps from the previous workout. The HIT system uses the double progressive technique and then adds a third component, time under tension—the total amount of time it takes to complete a set from start to finish. Adding the time component creates the *triple progressive* overload process, which is essential for measuring accurate strength gains, for reproducing perfect reps, and for eliminating cheating during the reps.

Triple Progressive Overload Technique

1. Increase time under tension
2. Increase reps
3. Increase weight—and do not cheat!

For the HIT system to be successful in developing maximal strength, athletes and coaches must understand how to properly implement the triple progressive overload technique by understanding each aspect.

Increasing Time Under Tension

Time under tension refers to the amount of time the muscle or muscles are being stressed during a set; the muscle should never relax at any time during the entire set. The recommended time under tension per rep is between five and seven seconds (see table 4.1).

Table 4.1 Time Under Tension for Rep Ranges

Sample rep range	Time under tension	Rounded off
6-8 reps	30-56 sec.	30-60 sec.
9-12 reps	45-84 sec.	45-90 sec.
12-16 reps	60-112 sec.	60-120 sec.
16-20 reps	80-140 sec.	80-140 sec.

Therefore, if an athlete sets a rep range between 10 and 12 reps, the time under tension range is between 50 seconds (10 reps × 5 seconds) and 84 seconds (12 reps × 7 seconds). For example, suppose an athlete executes 10 perfect reps to MMF on the leg extension machine with 100 pounds, and the total time under tension is 60 seconds. The average rep speed is calculated by dividing the 10 reps into 60 seconds, which equals an average of 6 seconds per rep. The recommendation for the next workout, assuming the rep range is 10 to 12, would be to stay with 100 pounds, increase the time under tension to more than 60 seconds, and increase the number of reps to 11 or 12.

The following example shows how an athlete can perform more reps but actually do less work. During Monday's workout the athlete uses 100 pounds on the leg extension machine and executes 10 reps in 60 seconds, for an average rep speed of 6 seconds. Two days later, the athlete uses 100 pounds again on the leg extension and performs 12 reps in 48 seconds. The average rep speed has dropped to 4 seconds. This is below the minimum 5-second guideline for acceptable perfect rep speed, and the total time under tension is 12 seconds less than the time under tension performed on Monday. The athlete, unfortunately, believes that strength gains have been achieved because two more reps have been performed than in the previous workout. However, because the time under tension was 12 seconds less and the resistance was the same, the athlete has not increased the overload. Instead, greater momentum was used and less work performed per rep. The athlete ended up with more reps and less quality of muscle tissue breakdown during the set.

A more effective approach would be to keep the weight at 100 pounds and try to exceed the time under tension of 60 seconds with the same number or greater number of reps. Most athletes are not aware of their rep speeds and will average 1.5 to 2 seconds per rep, but, as discussed in chapter 2, performing fast reps reduces muscle recruitment and limits the athlete's ability to maximize strength gains through the full range of motion.

The bottom line is that the HIT system is made up of specific guidelines that must be understood and practiced in order to properly develop workouts that progress for each subsequent training session to show strength improvements. It is therefore essential to accurately record each workout so that adjustments can be made to the weight, number of reps, and time under tension from workout to workout.

Of course, it is not practical to use a stopwatch to time every set; however, athletes and coaches are strongly encouraged to use a wristwatch to get an idea of how long each set takes to complete. It is critical that the athlete understand the importance of time under tension if the HIT system is going to be successful. When the athlete has fully matured into the HIT system, the rep tempo becomes automatic and using a stopwatch becomes unnecessary.

Increasing Reps With Time Under Tension Adjustments

The athlete will set a rep range, such as 10 to 12 reps, and then focus on reaching the high end of the range during the set. In addition, there must be a time under tension range that corresponds with the rep range. For example, an athlete may set a rep range from 10 to 12 reps, which would correspond with a time under tension range between 50 seconds (10 reps × 5 seconds) and 84 seconds (12 reps × 7 seconds). If the athlete performs 10 reps in 60 seconds, the average rep has been performed in 6 seconds. In the subsequent workout, the athlete may aim to reach 11 to 12 reps, with a time under tension greater than 60 seconds. If the athlete then performs 12 reps in 66 seconds, this shows an increase in time under tension per rep, with the average rep being greater than 5 seconds—an acceptable outcome.

Athletes should be motivated to increase the number of reps during every set; however, they should not compromise the time under tension variable or the perfect rep by adding more momentum to achieve a greater number of reps.

Increasing Weight

Once the athlete has reached maximum time under tension and rep range, it is time to increase the weight accordingly. The average increases—which should not compromise the athlete's ability to perform perfect reps within the rep range and time under tension—are usually between 5 and 10 percent of the weight lifted. A safe guideline for most athletes is generally a 5 percent increase for multijointed movements and a 10 percent increase for single-jointed movements. Typically, these increases will work fine if the athlete is beginning the off-season strength program, but if the athlete is close to reaching peak strength, the incremental increases will be significantly lower and less frequent.

The triple progressive overload process is the most effective way to accurately assess whether there have been valid strength gains because it accurately assesses the workload in a controlled lifting environment, versus one that deteriorates into less than perfect reps. It helps athletes understand the importance of the controlled rep, with guidelines that distinguish good reps from bad ones. Educated HIT athletes and coaches eventually become fanatical about good form and will accept nothing less. The ultimate payoff includes significantly fewer injuries while achieving maximal strength gains.

UNDERSTANDING MUSCLE TISSUE BREAKDOWN AND RECOVERY

Supercompensation is the "window of opportunity" when the muscle or muscles have completely recovered from an overload stimulus and are ready to be stimulated once again. The level of intensity, or magnitude of effort, dictates the level of muscle tissue breakdown and the period of time that is required for complete recovery before the next strength training stimulus occurs. Understanding this concept is imperative for athletes who want to reach their maximum strength potential and avoid overtraining.

Figure 4.1, the supercompensation graph, illustrates the average amount of recovery time needed for muscle tissue repair according to the level of overload on the muscles. If an athlete is performing exercise sets that do not produce significant amounts of lactic acid, which causes muscle fatigue, the muscles are performing light, non-MMF exercises. For example, suppose an athlete performs 35 push-ups and then stops, when she could have performed 50 to failure; or suppose another athlete performs 10 reps on the bench press with a weight he could have completed to 15 reps to MMF. These examples reflect light overloads that do not break down the muscle tissue to the point that it needs more than 24 hours' recovery. When

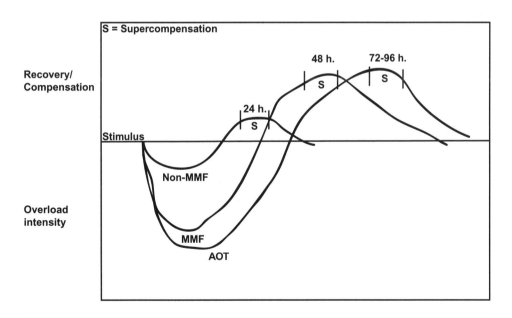

Figure 4.1 Intensity and supercompensation: intensity of overload versus recovery time. Deeper muscle tissue breakdown requires a longer recovery period in order to avoid overtraining.

an athlete begins to perform sets to MMF, it becomes necessary to give the muscle a minimum of 48 hours for the tissue to completely recover. If the athlete performs advanced overload techniques, which further increase the level of muscle tissue breakdown, the recovery period must be a minimum of 72 to 96 hours. If the athlete trains before the muscle tissue has completely healed, then overtraining symptoms start to appear, injury potential increases, maximum strength gains are not accomplished, and eventually training stops.

Level of Intensity

Many athletes begin the HIT program with little awareness of the true meaning of MMF. Some athletes do not have a high tolerance for muscular discomfort. MMF is a relative term and is dictated by each athlete's ability to push to the highest possible levels of discomfort during a set. An athlete who has a low tolerance for muscle discomfort and performs a set to perceived failure—a subjective judgment—will be under the illusion of having reached MMF. The HIT system teaches athletes how to increase their tolerance for muscular discomfort and tap into the deepest inroads of muscle fiber tissue recruitment. On the other hand, athletes who have a high tolerance for muscle discomfort and the ability to tap into the deepest inroads of muscle fiber tissue gain the greatest amount of strength over time. The HIT system focuses on high-intensity work using a low volume of sets and exercises. The system builds athletes' mental toughness and physical tolerance for muscle discomfort; in addition, it builds discipline and self-confidence, which many athletes have found beneficial on the field of play.

The body's chief source of energy for short duration, high-intensity anaerobic exercise is adenosine triphosphate-creatine phosphate (ATP-CP). During a strength training set, ATP-CP and glycogen are the primary sources of energy for the muscles and are replenished when the muscles rest between sets. During a set to MMF, ATP-CP is being reduced in the muscle and anaerobic glycolysis is producing lactic acid, which will eventually shut the muscle down. Either the athlete will stop, if the muscle discomfort becomes too much, or the muscle will reach MMF and shut down. As the athlete's tolerance for the muscle discomfort caused by lactic acid accumulation increases, deeper inroads of muscle breakdown can be achieved. The HIT system enhances the athlete's ability to work at high levels of lactic acid accumulation. This process improves the athlete's anaerobic threshold, known as $\dot{V}O_2max$, thereby allowing the athlete to produce high energy output with a faster recovery period.

Over the past 10 years the NSPA has collected data on hundreds of athletes using heart rate (HR) as an indicator of intensity while performing HIT strength training sets. The data show that the HR increases according to the athlete's ability to push to a higher level of muscle discomfort. In fact, the HR was found to be relative to the person's tolerance for muscle discomfort and was not age related.

NSPA uses HR as a tool to motivate athletes. When athletes wear the heart rate monitor, they are notified of their HR during each set, and it becomes apparent that they are motivated to push beyond the HRs previously recorded for them for each exercise. Interestingly, the average HR to MMF remains the same, regardless of number of reps beyond 6 or the type of exercise, whether squats or biceps curls. Monitoring HR during training is yet another effective way to help athletes increase intensity, thereby affecting the level of muscle tissue breakdown and degree of improved strength (see figure 4.2).

Advanced Overload Training

As athletes mature into the HIT system, they build a higher tolerance for muscle discomfort, as discussed previously, and some athletes look for ways to extend a set or make it more difficult. These methods are called *advanced overload training* (AOT). They include the following: pre- and postexhaustion, breakdowns, assisted positives, forced negatives, and isometric pauses. When an athlete uses AOT, a minimum of 72 to 96 recovery hours are required to make sure that the muscle tissue has completely repaired.

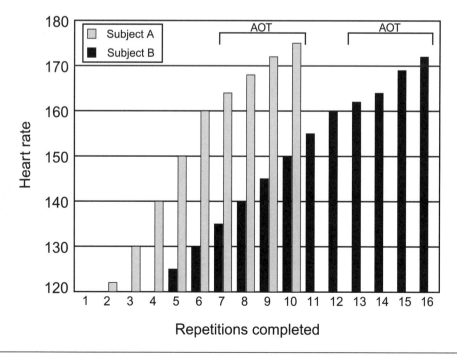

Figure 4.2 Intensity and heart rate. Though rep ranges to MMF are different, the heart rate levels achieved are similar.

Athletes should use AOT sparingly and be careful not to get carried away with certain muscle groups, like the chest and biceps. The use of AOT applications is recommended once an athlete has reached a plateau performing MMF sets. If an athlete feels compelled to use AOT on a regular basis, it is best to train each body part only twice per week in order to allow a minimum of three to four recovery days. Athletes must remember not to train one muscle group with greater intensity or volume than another—for example, overbenching for the chest without working the post delts equally, or overemphasizing the quads without giving equal attention to the hamstrings—because this will eventually lead to muscle imbalance. Every athlete should strive for a balanced training program.

HOW MANY SETS?

How many sets are necessary for gains in strength? This question is possibly the most heavily debated topic among strength and conditioning coaches across the country, and there are just as many research articles supporting the one-set protocol as there are supporting the multiple-set protocols.

The original Nautilus one-set principle has been successfully used by athletes for more than 30 years and continues to be effective for people participating in all levels of sport. One-set training involves higher levels of intensity, less volume, and fewer training sessions. The key to using the one-set protocol is making sure that athletes perform each perfect set to MMF and that the overload stimulus is equal to or greater than that of the previous workout. Consequently, athletes must have the mental toughness to push beyond their previous best and then maintain that level of intensity once they have reached their athletic strength potential.

Many HIT practitioners incorporate multiple sets into their strength training programs. A second or third set, if done correctly, can potentially achieve deeper inroads into the muscle tissue as long as MMF occurs with each set. Multiple sets are often beneficial if a facility has limited equipment and exercise choices. Table 4.2 illustrates a traditional multiple-set protocol versus the HIT multiple-set protocol. In this example, the warm-up sets have been completed and the three sets represent the progressive overload sets, or working sets, with a 90-second recovery period between sets.

The traditional protocol uses a greater weight with each consecutive set. The first and second sets do not reach MMF, so additional warm-up sets are a waste of time and energy. In fact, if an athlete performs 12 exercises for the upper body and uses this protocol for each exercise, the total number of warm-up sets would be 24. This traditional, non-HIT protocol is not efficient strength training for an athlete.

The HIT protocol uses enough weight on the first set to reach MMF within the desired rep range. During each additional set, the athlete reaches MMF.

Table 4.2 Traditional Versus HIT Multiple-Set Protocols

Traditional multiple-set protocol				HIT advanced overload protocol			
Weight	×	Reps	Time under tension	Weight	×	Reps	Time under tension
80	×	10	15 sec.	100	×	10	70 sec. (MMF)
90	×	10	15 sec.	100	×	8	48 sec. (MMF)
100	×	10	15 sec. (P-MMF)	100	×	6	30 sec. (MMF)

Rep range 6-10 reps; MMF = positive momentary muscular failure; P-MMF = perceived MMF

Whereas under the traditional protocol the athlete performed the third set to "perceived" P-MMF in 15 seconds, with an average rep speed of 1.5, the athlete following the HIT protocol performs three sets to 100 percent MMF, totaling 2 minutes 45 seconds under tension for an average rep speed of 6.0. The HIT protocol is far more demanding and intense than the traditional protocol and therefore elicits greater strength gains.

Multiple sets can be used to create variety in workouts. The use of multiple sets decreases the total number of exercises in a given workout but will not affect the total number of sets. For example, table 4.3 shows three different, complete upper body workouts, with a total of 14 sets for each workout.

Table 4.3 One-, Two-, and Three-Set Routines

1-Set routine (14 exercises)	2-Set routine (8 exercises)	3-Set routine (6 exercises)
Lat pulldown (M)	Lat pulldown (M)	Lat pulldown (M)
Lat pullover (S)	Lat pulldown (M)	Lat pulldown (M)
Chest press (M)	Chest press (M)	Lat pulldown (M)
Chest cross (S)	Chest press (M)	Chest press (M)
Seated row (M)	Seated row (M)	Chest press (M)
Iso seated row (S)	Seated row (M)	Chest press (M)
Seated press (M)	Seated press (M)	Seated row (M)
Lateral raise (S)	Seated press (M)	Seated row (M)
Incline row (M)	Incline row (M)	Seated row (M)
Iso incline row (S)	Incline row (M)	Seated press (M)
Incline press (M)	Incline press (M)	Seated press (M)
Incline cross (S)	Incline press (M)	Seated press (M)
Biceps curl (S)	Biceps curl (S)	Biceps curl (S)
Triceps extension (S)	Triceps extension (S)	Triceps extension (S)

(S) = Single-joint exercise; (M) = Multijoint exercise

> ### HIT Programming Suggestions
>
> Before beginning the HIT program, athletes should perform a 5- to 10-minute cardio-vascular warm-up and then 5 to 10 minutes of static stretching of the muscle groups that will be targeted. The HIT system only requires one good warm-up set for the joints before the first exercise; however, some athletes might need to perform two or maybe three warm-up sets because of past injuries or psychological comfort level. In addition, if the first exercise is a single-joint movement, an additional warm-up set is recommended before the first multijoint movement, to make sure all joints are ready for MMF. Once the warm-up set is complete and the joints are prepared, every subsequent set is performed to MMF. In other words, there are no more warm-up sets! Chapter 5 will describe in detail all of the ways the HIT programs add variety to the strength routines.

REP RANGES FOR MAXIMUM RESULTS

Most athletes are taught at a very young age that heavier weights and lower reps will make them big and strong, whereas lighter weights and higher reps will give them strength endurance. This concept has some truth to it; however, genetic strength factors become a significant influence on how athletes will respond to any type of strength training. Table 4.4 contains general strength guidelines for rep ranges and time under tension. For sport-specific rep ranges, refer to chapter 8.

If a male high school football player and a female basketball player wanted to gain strength to improve their athletic performance, each would aim for a rep range of 6 to 12 reps. A long-distance runner would aim for a rep range of 14 and 20 reps, occasionally testing his strength endurance with reps to MMF between 20 and 40.

Unless an athlete is a competitive power lifter or Olympic lifter, there is no need to perform one to three reps to failure with maximum loads. The HIT system does not test the one-rep maximum to figure out the

Table 4.4 General Strength Guidelines for Reps and Time Under Tension

General strength goal	Rep range	Time under tension range (based on 6-sec. average)
Competitive lifting	1-3 reps (high injury risk)	6-18 sec.
Strength	6-12 reps	36-72 sec.
Strength endurance	14-20 reps	84-120 sec.
Max strength endurance	20-40 reps	2-4 min.

necessary weight needed to start a particular exercise or to estimate the percentage needed for specific cycles when following a periodization model. Instead, the HIT system tests the athlete's strength during every exercise performed to MMF, within a safe rep range. The number one rule in the weight room is safety and injury prevention. Any injury in the weight room is unacceptable.

Some athletes might believe that larger-framed, heavier athletes, such as linemen, must perform different rep ranges from smaller-framed, lighter athletes, such as gymnasts. This is not true. Many sports, such as wrestling or boxing, have designated weight classes. Regardless of weight class, each athlete uses the same strength program. In other words, the same rep ranges, sets, recovery, and exercises are recommended for both types of athletes.

Dr. Wayne Westcott performed a study with 87 men and women to see how many reps they could perform to failure with 75 percent of their one-rep maximum on the leg extension. As figure 4.3 illustrates, a majority of the subjects performed 8 to 13 reps; this indicates an even distribution of fast-twitch and slow-twitch muscle fibers. Sixteen of the subjects, successful power athletes, performed fewer than 8 reps. It is safe to assume that they have predominantly fast-twitch muscle fibers. Finally, 17 of the subjects performed more than 13 repetitions. These people were all outstanding endurance athletes, and it is assumed that they have predominantly slow-twitch, high-endurance muscle fibers.

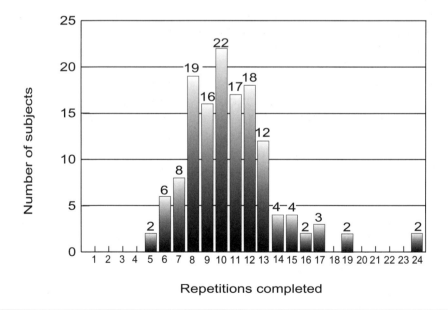

Figure 4.3   Studies indicate that most subjects have an even distribution of fast- and slow-twitch fibers. Power athletes in this study performed fewer than eight reps and probably have fast-twitch fibers, and endurance athletes performed more reps and likely have more slow-twitch fibers.

RECOVERY TIME BETWEEN SETS

Another variable for manipulating intensity during sets is the recovery time between sets. The average HIT recovery time between sets is approximately 90 seconds. A majority of athletes are not aware of their recovery time between sets, which typically averages three to four minutes. Many times three athletes work together, which is very ineffective because recovery periods between sets can be four to five minutes in length. No more than two athletes should lift together, and both should be conscious of recovery times between sets.

Recovery intervals between sets can be manipulated to induce certain physiological training responses, such as an increased anaerobic threshold. The HIT system allows approximately 90 seconds of recovery, which will replenish approximately 90 to 100 percent of the ATP-CP in the muscle of a well-conditioned athlete. Keep in mind that this replenishment is based on MMF alone and not AOT. Athletes may at first find it difficult to get through a full HIT workout with only 90 seconds of recovery between sets. However, after several weeks of using the HIT system, athletes become more efficient at transporting oxygen to the working muscles and can intensify the workout with less perceived effort. Consequently, they build a tolerance for high-intensity training and can push harder but recover quickly.

An endurance athlete or golfer looking to lose weight and increase strength could use a circuit training approach designed to elevate the training heart rate and maintain it above 60 percent of max heart rate during the entire workout. A full body strength routine, to be performed twice a week, would consist of one set of 12 to 16 reps performed to MMF for each of 10 to 12 exercises. The recovery between sets would be 30 to 60 seconds, for a total workout time of approximately 25 minutes or less. This routine would increase strength, as long as there was consistent overload, and would have some cardiovascular benefit if the heart rate stayed above 60 percent of the max heart rate for the entire 25 minutes of the workout. On the other hand, if a female shot-putter were looking for maximum strength gains for explosive power, she should perform 4 to 8 reps to MMF with 2 to 2.5 minutes of recovery after each set.

The following table, referenced from another study conducted by Dr. Westcott, presents a time progression of muscle energy replenishment. These are expressed as approximate percentages of ATP-CP after a set of 10 HIT reps to complete muscle failure on the leg extension machine. These subjects were from the general population. As athletes get in better shape, the recovery of ATP-CP is higher than the percentages presented in table 4.5.

Table 4.5   Replenishment of Muscle Energy Stores

Recovery time	Approximate percentage of ATP-CP replacement
30 sec.	50
1 min.	75
90 sec.	87.5
2 min.	93.7
2½ min.	96.8
3 min.	98.4
4 min.	99.6
5 min.	99.9

Reprinted with permission from Wayne Westcott, *Strength Fitness,* 4th ed. (Dubuque: Brown and Benchmark, 1995).

GAS AND OVERTRAINING

In 1956, a scientist by the name of Hans Selye developed a theory called the general adaptation syndrome (GAS), which is essentially an elaborated version of Nietzsche's famous claim that "that which does not kill us makes us stronger." The GAS theory is directly related to the overload process and strength training. During the first stage, or alarm stage, a physiological and metabolic stress is applied to the muscle tissue, causing microscopic damage. During the second stage, the adaptation stage, the body defends itself against the overload by repairing itself and increasing in size and strength. This is recognized as "compensatory adaptation" and muscle hypertrophy; however, if the stress is excessive or too severe, it can create a catabolic effect. In this situation the muscle or muscles are broken down in such an extreme manner that the body cannot effectively regenerate muscle tissue—it cannot resynthesize myofibril proteins—and adapt. In a case like this, the body induces a third stage, the overtraining stage, which is first manifested through subtle signs. If the workouts continue to be too intense, too long, or both, then the overtraining symptoms become much more severe and may lead to serious overtraining injuries.

Subtle overtraining symptoms

▸ Elevation in morning heart rate or blood pressure

▸ Lack of appetite, weight loss, or thirst

▸ Lack of physical energy or lethargy

▸ Illness, colds, flu, or low resistance (suppression of immune system)

▸ Reduced quality of sleep or difficulty falling asleep
▸ Psychological stress:
  ▸ Inability to maintain focus or concentrate
  ▸ No enthusiasm or drive to work out
▸ Diminished strength and athletic performance
▸ Muscle cramps or trigger points
▸ Mild soft-tissue and joint soreness

Serious overtraining symptoms

▸ Excessive soft-tissue and joint tenderness
▸ Connective tissue inflammation or tears
▸ Excessive weight loss
▸ Muscle pulls
▸ Joint instability
▸ Injury requiring surgery

When signs of overtraining occur, the coach and athlete should immediately address the symptoms and figure out solutions to remedy the problem and prevent further progression of symptoms. They must review in detail the entire physical training program, including the frequency, intensity, and volume of work; all outside psychological stressors, such as family, relationships, work, school, and finances; and recovery components, such as sleep, nutrition, hydration, and other physical activities. If the athlete is a minor, parents should be involved in the discussion. Athletes often become overwhelmed by outside stressors that have a direct impact on the training program. The best solution is to analyze all components and list specific task-oriented objectives to follow to get back on track.

This chapter has presented some significant changes in strength training applications and methodologies when compared to the more traditional strength training approaches. The goal has been to provide new and exciting information for your strength training toolbox. You should now have a better understanding of the overload process and the importance of time under tension as a third component for the triple progressive overload lifting protocol. You should be conscious of performing perfect reps, of recovery time between sets, of the number of working sets, of performing sets to MMF, and of implementing AOT to maximize genetic athletic strength potential. Most important, you should now be aware of how HIT builds a foundation of balanced strength and allows athletes to achieve their maximum athletic strength potential in half of the time it takes most traditional strength systems. This allows more time for sport-specific skill acquisition and practice.

Periodization Plan for the HIT Program

Periodization involves the planning and integration of numerous conditioning components for a defined period and is typically used to peak for athletic competition. The time frame for a periodization plan may be as long as four years to lead up to competition at the Olympic Games or as short as an eight-week training camp for a world championship boxing match. Periodization plans include a wide range of conditioning components, such as aerobic and anaerobic conditioning, sport-specific skills, flexibility, strength, speed and power development, agility, and balance. Modifications in the daily lifestyle of the athlete, such as enhanced nutrition, hydration, and recovery protocols, are also considered an important part of a periodization plan. Recovery for athletes during this time frame may include ice baths, contrast therapy (from ice to heat to ice), massage, and additional hours of sleep.

When athletes follow a periodization plan that includes the HIT system, the training program can be designed to maximize strength gains during the preseason, throughout the entire season, and into the postseason playoffs. Although many athletic seasons last five months or longer, athletes must be at their peak athletic strength during the preseason to make the team and to protect themselves from injury. In addition, athletes must maintain this peak strength throughout the season and into the playoffs. Unlike the athletes of years ago, today's athletes must strength train no less than 11 months out of the year to maintain their highest level of athletic performance. The HIT system is also effective for athletes who play two or three different sports during the year, as well as for those who play sports that have two or three games per week during the season. This chapter will present a year-round HIT periodization plan that is applicable for all sports.

A vital training component for the success of the HIT program and periodization plan is to keep accurate records for every workout. It is critical that the athlete clearly show results with proper documentation. In addition to color-coded workout cards, many HIT practitioners find computer software programs such as Electric Coach to be very useful. Accountable records are kept for the following reasons:

▸ To track the percentage of strength lost during the postseason recovery phase

▸ To track specific progress from one workout and one exercise to the next

▸ To track the percentage of strength increase during each strength phase

▸ To maintain records of best efforts for each exercise for each full season

▸ To accurately assess any change or decrease in strength that might indicate overuse or overtraining

▸ To maintain records of strength progression in case of injury or illness

This chapter describes in detail each periodization phase and its goals and provides a lifting schedule for each. The year-round plan includes lifting schedules for the off-season, preseason, in-season, and postseason strength phases, as well as the off-season recovery phase.

OFF-SEASON STRENGTH PHASE

The goal of the off-season strength phase, which lasts between 18 and 22 weeks, is to rebuild strength that was lost during the two- to four-week off-season recovery phase. In general, athletes lose 12 to 20 percent of their strength during the off-season recovery phase. Over the last 18 years, NSPA has developed thousands of strength periodization programs for athletes, from 16 to 40 years old, participating in a variety of sports at all levels. The accumulated data shown in table 5.1 reflect the average strength loss during the off-season recovery phase. These data can be used to figure out starting weights at the beginning of the off-season strength phase.

Finding the starting weight for each exercise is not as complicated as you might think, and involves the following steps:

1. Calculate how many weeks were spent without lifting.
2. Figure out the average percentage of loss from last year's best effort (see table 5.1).

Table 5.1 Average Strength Loss Per Week

Post-recovery period	Average strength loss
*10 days-3 weeks	4-8%
3-4 weeks	8-12%
4-5 weeks	12-16%
5-6 weeks	16-20%
6-7 weeks	20-24%
7-8 weeks	24-28%
*8-10 weeks	28-32%
10-12 weeks	32-40%

* NSPA recommends taking off no more than 4 – 6 weeks from strength training primarily due to the amount of strength loss that will occur during weeks 8 through 12.

3. Use the formula in table 5.2 to estimate the amount of weight needed, or refer to your strength training records from the previous year and figure out the athlete's average strength loss.

For example, let's assume an athlete's best effort at the end of the season for a specified exercise, such as the leg press machine, was 300 pounds × 10 reps. Factor in the number of weeks without lifting, and find the average percentage of strength loss in table 5.1. Then multiply the percentage of strength loss by the best effort from last year to determine the estimated starting weight. The average athlete will not begin to lose strength until 8 to 12 days after the last lifting session.

In general, the goal for the first week of strength training during the off-season strength phase is to assess the current strength level and reestablish perfect rep form. Athletes should start by executing 12 to 15 perfect reps to the point of muscle discomfort but not to MMF. Within the

Table 5.2 Formula for Estimating Off-Season Starting Weight

Weeks off	Last year's best effort	×	Estimated percentage of strength loss	=	Estimated starting weight (rounded off)
2-3	300 lbs.	×	90% (10% loss/3 wk.)	=	270 lbs.
3-4	300 lbs.	×	85% (15% loss/4 wk.)	=	255 lbs.
4-5	300 lbs.	×	80% (20% loss/5 wk.)	=	240 lbs.
5-6	300 lbs.	×	75% (25% loss/6 wk.)	=	225 lbs.

first few reps, if the weight is too heavy or too light, stop immediately and adjust the weight accordingly. During the second week, athletes should execute 10 to 12 reps (or more, if appropriate), to MMF. During the third week, athletes are ready to achieve MMF within the appropriate rep range for their personal strength goals.

Historically, NSPA has found that most athletes starting the off-season strength phase will experience the highest percentage of strength gains during their first two to three weeks of training. This is primarily due to neuromuscular reeducation as the muscles relearn motor skills. Muscle has memory and will quickly reestablish the necessary motor pathways to make exercises more efficient. This neurological reeducation immediately increases strength, as opposed to building pure metabolic strength. Athletes should choose two workout routines, one for the upper body and one for the lower body, to use during the first two weeks to reestablish MMF. Additional routines should be added during the third week.

The goal is to rebuild strength with every exercise in the first four weeks and then to reach the previous year's best effort. When the previous year's best efforts have been reestablished, it is time to take that effort to a higher level—to get bigger, faster, and stronger.

Tables 5.3 and 5.4 show the average strength gains for NSPA athletes over the past 18 years. Keep in mind that these percentages are an average; individual athletes must factor in their genetic predisposition, their maturation level, the number of years they've been lifting, the number of years they've used the HIT program, the number of weeks they've gone without lifting, the frequency of their lifting sessions, the level of intensity, and the specific exercise. Athletes will see the most gains in the first two weeks because of the neurological reeducation discussed previously. The average strength gain during the first six to eight weeks is approximately 5 to 6 percent per week, then tapers down to 2 to 3 percent per week until peak strength levels are reached. Of course, at this point the goal is to slowly break through the plateau to reach individual peak strength levels.

Table 5.3 Average Strength Gains

Date		12/20/02	1/20/03
Exercise	Seat	Best effort	Wt. × Reps
4-way neck	4	80 × 12	60 × 12
Pulldown	6	240 × 10	210 × 12
Pulldown	6	240 × 8	210 × 10
Free bench	—	265 × 10	225 × 10

Table 5.4 Weekly Average Strength Gains for the Off-Season Strength Phase

Weeks	Average strength gain
2	8-12%
3	12-16%
4	16-20%
5	20-24%
6	24-28%
7	28-32%
8	32-36%
9	36-40%
10	40-44%

OFF-SEASON LIFTING SCHEDULE

If an athlete does not lift for three to four weeks during the off-season recovery phase, the following weekly schedule will help accelerate the strength rebuilding process during the beginning of the off-season strength phase. This schedule involves three upper body lifts and three lower body lifts. Keep in mind that the first two weeks are designed to reestablish perfect form and determine the appropriate weights to achieve MMF.

Three-day split—three days upper and three days lower. Options 1 and 2 are ideal for those athletes who have the time to work out every day except for one (see table 5.5). The rest day does not have to be Sunday. The upper body workout consists of 12 to 16 total sets, which should take 40 to 45 minutes, according to the following formula: The average set of 10 reps takes 60 seconds to complete, plus 90 seconds of recovery between each set, totals 2 minutes 30 seconds; 2 minutes 30 seconds (time under tension plus recovery) multiplied by 16 exercises yields 40 minutes total workout time.

This workout does not include four-way neck exercises, which should be incorporated into the program if the sport involves contact. This would add an additional four sets and 8 to 10 minutes to the routine. If neck machines are limited, manual resistance can be used with large groups. The lower body workout, including a set of lower back extensions to MMF, will consist of 12 to 16 sets and last 40 to 45 minutes.

Options 1 and 2 are recommended for use during the beginning of the off-season only, while athletes are rebuilding strength to reach their best

Table 5.5 Off-Season Lifting Schedule for Accelerated Strength Building

3-Day split—3 days upper/3 days lower						
	Monday	**Tuesday**	**Wednesday**	**Thursday**	**Friday**	**Saturday**
Option 1	Upper 12-16 sets	Lower 12-16 sets	Upper 12-16 sets	Lower 12-16 sets	Upper 12-16 sets	Lower 12-16 sets
Option 2	Lower 12-16 sets	Upper 12-16 sets	Lower 12-16 sets	Upper 12-16 sets	Lower 12-16 sets	Upper 12-16 sets
Full body						
	Monday	**Tuesday**	**Wednesday**	**Thursday**	**Friday**	**Saturday**
Option 3	Full body 24-26 sets		Full body 24-26 sets		Full body 24-26 sets	
Option 4		Full body 24-26 sets		Full body 24-26 sets		Full body 24-26 sets

efforts from the previous year. It is recommended that the athlete does a two-day split every third week while on this lifting schedule. This will prevent overtraining. Any AOT beyond MMF should be performed during the last two days of the six-day training period to allow for a minimum of three recovery days before the next workout. As discussed in chapter 4, AOT breaks down the muscle tissue beyond the standard one set or multiple sets to MMF and requires a minimum of three to four days of structured recovery.

Full body—three days upper and three days lower. The full body workout consists of three days in the weight room per week and requires performing approximately 24 to 26 total sets in 60 to 75 total workout minutes. The abdominals, neck, and lower back must be trained during each workout. These exercises are included in the 24 to 26 sets. As in the split routine, AOT should only be applied on Friday or Saturday to allow for a minimum of three days' recovery. This reduces the risk of overtraining.

Similar to the split routine, this schedule is effective during the first 6 to 10 weeks of the off-season strength phase if the athlete has not lifted during the 3- to 4-week off-season recovery phase. If, however, the athlete has not lifted for 6 to 8 weeks, then the accelerated strength building schedule should be extended. Another popular approach to the off-season weekly schedule is to focus three days on the upper body and three days on the lower body one week, followed by two days on the upper body and two days on the lower body the next week. This schedule ensures additional recovery and allows athletes to perform AOT and then get plenty of recovery. Once the previous year's best effort has been achieved, use the pre- and in-season lifting schedule.

PRESEASON AND IN-SEASON STRENGTH PHASES

The preseason strength phase, which lasts four to six weeks, focuses on maintaining the strength that was built during the off-season phase and, if possible, continuing to build on the previous year's best effort. Most preseason training camps are physically and mentally demanding, and maintaining strength through two practices a day can be very challenging. However, athletes must strength train during this time, even if only for 25 to 30 minutes four times a week, focusing two days on the upper body and two days on the lower. Some programs do not emphasize strength training at all during the preseason because of demanding practice schedules, so the athletes inevitably lose strength before the start of the season, as indicated in table 5.1. Therefore, it is essential for athletes and coaches to block out specific times in the busy preseason schedule for strength training. Do not assume that sport-specific practices will maintain strength levels; they will not! Strength training is the *only* way to maintain peak strength levels.

The goal during the preseason is to perform two upper body and two lower body strength sessions per week, each lasting 25 to 30 minutes, but this should be modified if the legs are being overworked with long, difficult practices. In this case, a minimum of one leg workout per week would maintain strength levels for several weeks. The number of exercises and sets can be reduced if recovery and energy expenditure are a concern. The athlete may, instead, want to consider performing two full body strength workouts of 12 to 14 sets per week, totaling 30 to 40 minutes each. If minor injuries occur to either the upper or lower extremities, the athlete can still maintain strength of the core muscles by performing single-joint exercises that avoid the injury or by using manual strength training techniques. See chapter 11 for more on manual exercises.

The in-season strength phase, which lasts 12 to 20 weeks, must be a priority with all athletes and coaches to maintain the strength that was built in the off-season. Many athletes who are still maturing physically or maturing within the HIT system are able to continue to increase their strength gains during the season. If an athlete stops lifting because of time constraints or a coach does not encourage lifting during the in-season, the athlete's strength levels will diminish significantly each week, regardless of sport-specific conditioning done during practice.

The primary goal of the in-season strength phase is to make sure that the strength levels achieved during the off-season phase are maintained and ideally improved throughout the entire competitive season. The HIT system enables athletes to maintain strength by lifting twice per week, full body, in only 40 minutes per training session, or to increase strength by using AOT once a week. Many HIT strength coaches have had success strength training athletes just once a week, upper and lower, during the last month of the regular season to maintain the athlete's peak strength. In fact, the bottom line is that once an athlete has reached peak strength, it is a function of keeping the same intensity, same weights, same reps, same time of tension, and more recovery, even with reduced training frequency.

PRESEASON AND IN-SEASON LIFTING SCHEDULES

Peak athletic strength can be maintained throughout the entire preseason and in-season with the optional schedules in table 5.6. Athletes and teams that do not follow these recommendations for strength training during the season tend to lose a strength-based edge in the later part of the season, which has a significant negative effect on their success.

Sunday is a common day off for most athletes. But some athletic teams must practice or compete on Sundays because of the demands of their sport and competition schedule. The strength program needs to be adjusted to accommodate this situation and to allow for adequate recovery before competition. Any athlete who is not experiencing postgame physical trauma should perform a full body workout to MMF the day after a competition to aid the recovery process.

Two-day split—two days upper and two days lower. This schedule has been very successful for athletes who push themselves and perform AOT once a week. This schedule encourages a minimum of three days of active recovery, which includes stretching, proper nutrition, adequate hydration, and sleep. Athletes who strength-train on a year-round basis and only take off one to two weeks during the year find this lifting schedule very favorable for maintaining and improving strength levels year in and year out.

Full body split—two days upper and two days lower. This lifting schedule option is successful for maintaining strength when athletes have matched their best efforts from the previous year and want to continue increasing strength. This lifting schedule allows for maximum recovery, especially if the athlete is performing AOT once a week.

Full body. This lifting schedule is ideal for preseason and in-season lifting, especially for high school and college athletes with limited time. It allows for maximum recovery and the ability to maintain strength levels throughout the season. Keep in mind that athletes using the HIT system for the first time and athletes who are still going through the maturation process will continue to make strength gains during the season. It is essential that all teams continue strength training during the season. "If you don't use it, you will lose it!" Realistically, the athlete and coach need to schedule only two hours per week to train for strength maintenance. If they do not, the athlete will experience significant strength losses before the end of the season and especially during the postseason playoffs.

Table 5.6 Preseason and In-Season Lifting Schedule

2-Day split—2 days upper/2 days lower						
	Monday	**Tuesday**	**Wednesday**	**Thursday**	**Friday**	**Saturday**
Option 1	Upper 12-16 sets	Lower 12-16 sets		Upper 12-16 sets	Lower 12-16 sets	
Option 2	Lower 12-16 sets	Upper 12-16 sets		Lower 12-16 sets	Upper 12-16 sets	
Option 3		Upper 12-16 sets	Lower 12-16 sets		Upper 12-16 sets	Lower 12-16 sets
Option 4		Lower 12-16 sets	Upper 12-16 sets		Upper 12-16 sets	Lower 12-16 sets
Full body split—2 days upper/2 days lower						
	Monday	**Tuesday**	**Wednesday**	**Thursday**	**Friday**	**Saturday**
Option 5	Full body 24-26 sets			Full body 24-26 sets		
	Upper 12-16 sets	Lower 12-16 sets		Upper 12-16 sets	Lower 12-16 sets	
Full body						
	Monday	**Tuesday**	**Wednesday**	**Thursday**	**Friday**	**Saturday**
Option 6	Full body 24-26 sets			Full body 24-26 sets		
Option 7		Full body 24-26 sets			Full body 24-26 sets	
Option 8			Full body 24-26 sets			Full body 24-26 sets
Full body split—2 days upper/2 days lower						
	Monday	**Tuesday**	**Wednesday**	**Thursday**	**Friday**	**Saturday**
Option 9	Full body 24-26 sets			Upper 12-16 sets	Lower 12-16 sets	
Option 10	Full body 24-26 sets			Lower 12-16 sets	Upper 12-16 sets	
Option 11	Lower 12-16 sets	Upper 12-16 sets			Full body 24-26 sets	
Option 12	Upper 12-16 sets	Lower 12-16 sets			Full body 24-26 sets	

Full body split—two days upper and two days lower. This lifting schedule allows a three- to four-day recovery period for all muscle groups. This is another popular and successful schedule for pre- and in-season strength phases.

As you can see, the HIT system incorporates variety not only through different lifting techniques but also through optional schedules. The result of the variety inherent to this training system is greater stimulation for both the body and the mind. There should be no excuses for any athlete or coach not to be able to find time during the week to continue peak strength.

POSTSEASON STRENGTH PHASE

During the end-of-season and postseason playoffs, which usually last one to three weeks, the emphasis is on maintaining peak strength while maximizing recovery. If this time frame is only two to four weeks long, athletes might respond better to one upper and one lower strength session per week to maintain strength and have adequate recovery. The body has the ability to maintain peak strength levels with one HIT workout a week for a period of weeks during the end of the regular season and into postseason playoffs. During this time, athletes and coaches should focus on short, quality practices; optimum nutrition; plenty of water; and adequate rest. It is better for athletes to be overrested at this stage than overtrained from a long season. The schedule in table 5.7 focuses on increased recovery and reduced volume of work while maintaining high intensity and peak athletic strength.

These weekly schedules have been very successful when used by athletes who train at a high intensity year round. In addition, many of the top NFL and college strength coaches throughout the country have found that athletes can maintain peak strength with one HIT session per week for three to four weeks toward the end of a season. Some athletes can maintain peak strength even longer. These options allow for four to seven days of recovery by alternating option 1, which incorporates two days of lower body work and one day of upper body work in one week, with option 2 the following week—one day of lower body exercises and one day of upper body exercises. This schedule is recommended for athletes who have reached their strength potential but need more recovery from a demanding competitive schedule that causes wear and tear on their bodies. Many athletes find that this lifting schedule works well for the last two to three weeks of the in-season and into the postseason. Experience shows that strength will stay at peak levels with this schedule, but remember that it is effective only with those athletes who have reached their peak athletic strength and who push to MMF and use AOT on a regular basis.

Athletes may encounter outside variables that alter their lifting schedules, such as trips and family- or business-related commitments. The HIT

Table 5.7   End-of-Season and Postseason Lifting Schedule

Split: 2 days lower/1 day upper followed by 2 days upper/1 day lower					
	Monday	**Tuesday**	**Wednesday**	**Thursday**	**Friday**	**Saturday**
Option 1	Lower 12-16 sets		Upper 12-16 sets	Lower 12-16 sets		
	Upper 12-16 sets			Lower 12-16 sets	Upper 12-16 sets	
Split: 1 day upper/1 day lower					
	Monday	**Tuesday**	**Wednesday**	**Thursday**	**Friday**	**Saturday**
Option 2	Lower 12-16 sets			Upper 12-16 sets		
	Upper 12-16 sets		Lower 12-16 sets			

system offers many different options so that these types of situations do not interfere with an athlete's progress and dedication. Athletes who are maturing with the HIT system and have used its training techniques for at least a year become adept at determining the most beneficial schedule for their body and strength goals.

College and high school sports programs have had great success training the full body the day after a game, assuming there are no game-related injuries. In fact, experience shows that lifting after a game helps to alleviate muscle soreness and speed recovery time. Five- to eight-minute-long partial to full body ice baths are also recommended, with the water temperature between 55 and 58 degrees.

OFF-SEASON RECOVERY PHASE

Historically, off-season recovery meant no strength training for 12 to 14 weeks, but today's athletes must strength-train on a year-round basis—with the exception of two to four weeks during off-season—to be competitive and reach their strength potential. The off-season recovery phase is a time for athletes to physically and mentally recover from a long, demanding season. It is not a time for athletes to let down their guard or become lazy or undisciplined. In fact, this phase involves maximizing the athlete's recovery with proper eating habits, hydration, flexibility, plenty of sleep, and light aerobic and anaerobic conditioning. Details on recovery and nutrition are included in chapter 6. If body weight or fat is of concern, then an athlete may perform 25 to 30 minutes of cardiorespiratory exercise, such as biking, running, or playing basketball, three to five times a week. Unfortunately, the nutritional habits of some athletes make it difficult for them to stay on track during the off-season. Many athletes overindulge in certain foods that can add weight quickly, especially if their caloric intake exceeds their significantly reduced caloric expenditure.

Athletes who need to gain weight or build more muscle during the off-season should consume more calories than they burn on a daily basis and should consider taking a maximum of two weeks off from lifting. Athletes who experience joint soreness or who need to rehabilitate from minor injuries must individually determine when to reinitiate MMF strength training. In fact, many athletes strength-train during the off-season recovery period and simply build in long weekends or plan minivacations throughout the entire off-season but never stop lifting altogether.

Athletes who do not lift weights during the three- to four-week off-season recovery phase will lose 12 to 18 percent of their overall strength levels. Therefore, unless an athlete has an injury limitation, she should initiate strength training within the first three to four weeks of the off-season recovery phase. If strength training is not resumed by the fourth week and is delayed until the sixth or eighth week, the strength loss will be significant and the athlete will have to invest more time to match the previous year's best effort. This will likely detract from valuable time that could be spent on building strength levels that could possibly exceed the previous year. Of course, if an athlete does not strength-train for two or more months, his strength levels will gradually decline to his natural strength, which is the level of strength the athlete would have if he did not participate in a structured strength program on a regular basis. Experienced weightlifters who have trained consistently for three to four years might not reach their natural strength levels for four to five months, but will still lose an average of 40 percent of their overall strength with three months of no training.

The HIT periodization plan is not as complicated as it appears at first glance. A periodization program is simply an organized calendar that addresses all aspects of athletic training with specific time frames for athletic strength peaking and maintenance. The athlete's weekly lifting program schedule can be adjusted to any sport at any level. It allows the athlete to make adjustments, if necessary, to the lifting schedules to accommodate practices and games. This system also gives athletes latitude to make adjustments in the schedule to accommodate individual responses to the program. It allows flexibility in scheduling while maintaining peak strength during the pre- and in-season with minimum time spent in the weight room. Most important, the periodization program makes it easier for athletes to continue lifting throughout the season; those who fail to do so will lose strength and see their athletic performance decline. Regardless of the level of play, a well-planned periodization program is essential for maximizing athletic success and creating the competitive edge.

CHAPTER

6

Creating the Competitive Edge

After a HIT strength training session, the athlete's muscles and liver will be depleted of glycogen, the stored sugar that comes from complex carbohydrates. Oxygen transport is reduced and there is a general sense of overall fatigue. The athlete's body has experienced a successful HIT session and now requires recovery for optimal repair of muscle tissue to take place.

NUTRITION AND SLEEP GUIDELINES

Posttraining nutrition is important for replenishing muscle energy and aiding in cellular repair. Eating a balanced meal within an hour after training maximizes muscle energy replacement and minimizes fat storage. If this is not possible, athletes should consume a protein shake and piece of fruit within 20 minutes after training and be sure to stay fully hydrated by measuring the weight loss during the exercise session and matching that weight loss with water and electrolyte rehydration.

The athlete's challenge is to have four to six complete balanced meals every day, each composed of approximately 500 to 800 calories, 55 percent complex carbs, 25 to 35 percent polyunsaturated fat, and 15 to 20 percent complete protein.

Athletes should strive to never be hungry and never full. A good way to achieve this is to "graze" on four to six small, balanced meals daily. Doing so will fuel athletes' workouts and stabilize the body's blood sugar levels, thereby preventing extreme feelings of hunger, which often lead to poor food choices and overeating. Eating frequently is not always an easy task and often takes some planning; athletes should aim to prepare a meal plan each day in advance and adhere to it. The rewards of following a healthy meal plan will pay off with better training and athletic performance results. Every athlete should eat like an Olympic champion—and avoid the fast-food fat fix! To lose weight and gain muscle, the body needs proper fuel. Moderation becomes an important basic rule and applies to fast food, fatty food, fried food, and sweets.

Highly trained athletes can store twice as much muscle and liver glycogen as untrained athletes. Glycogen, which is the primary fuel for muscle contraction, is depleted during strength and anaerobic training.

Athletes need approximately .5 to .75 gram of protein per pound of body weight each day. If an athlete consumes more than the recommended amount and abuses protein supplements, those supplements could potentially sabotage the athlete's performance. Excessive protein intake is stored as fat, and the metabolic waste products, specifically uric acid crystals, can cause potential arthritic-like joint inflammation. To determine the amount of protein an athlete requires per day, use the following formula:

Weight in pounds $\times$ .60 = required grams of protein

A 200-pound male athlete would require the following:

200 $\times$ .60 = 120 grams of protein

To convert grams to calories, multiply the number of protein grams by 4—the number of calories per gram of protein:

120 grams of protein $\times$ 4 = 480 calories

Therefore, a 200-pound athlete would need to consume 480 of those calories from protein sources.

Skeletal muscle fibers are made up of approximately 75 to 80 percent water. An athlete's muscles will look like shriveled-up raisins if they are not kept well-hydrated and supported with balanced mineral supplements. Caffeinated beverages cause dehydration, and it has been shown that 1,000 milligrams of caffeine—the equivalent of three 12-ounce sodas plus four 8-ounce cups of coffee—can cause irregular heartbeats in healthy athletes. Combining excessive intake of caffeine with high-intensity training is considered a high-risk behavior because of increased blood pressure and risk of heart attack and stroke. An athlete who insists on drinking caffeinated beverages should add an additional 6 to 8 ounces of water to the daily intake for every 12 ounces of caffeine consumed. If the athlete feels thirsty, performance can be compromised by 15 to 25 percent. Can most athletes afford to sacrifice this much of their performance ability?

According to all the basic nutrition information, athletes should follow these pretraining guidelines every day:

▶ Two to three hours before lifting, have a pretraining snack that is approximately 300 calories of complex carbohydrates with 10 percent protein—for example, a whole-wheat low-fat bagel with low-fat cream cheese or a teaspoon of jelly, and a banana, pear, or apple.

▶ Sip 8 to 12 ounces of water and 4 to 6 ounces of an electrolyte drink, such as Gatorade, 20 minutes before strength training.

▶ Drink 8 to 12 ounces of water during the strength training workout. The majority of athletes are probably never properly hydrated during training. This can decrease overall performance by as much as 30 percent.

Balanced Daily Nutrition Plan

Athletes should get about 50 to 55 percent of their daily food intake from complex carbohydrates, which include rice, grains, fruits, vegetables, pastas, and baked potatoes with skin. Twenty to 25 percent should come from polyunsaturated fat, primarily from vegetable sources, olive oil, flaxseed oil, walnuts, and deep-water cold fish like salmon and tuna. The diet should include only 5 to 10 percent saturated fat, which is any fat that is solid at room temperature. Fifteen to 20 percent should be composed of protein, which is primarily from vegetable, fish, poultry, and red meat sources. Broken down into servings, that means an athlete should eat the following:

▶ 6 to 8 servings of **starches**—grain, rice, pasta, and potatoes

▶ 3 to 4 servings of **vegetables**—varied colors: green, yellow, orange, and white

▶ 2 to 4 servings of **fruit**—varied colors and fiber content

▶ 2 to 3 servings of low-fat **dairy**—primarily for calcium

▶ 2 to 3 servings of **protein**—fish, poultry, beans, and meat

▶ 64 to 96 ounces of **water**—*sipped* daily

© Human Kinetics

Athletes should find a healthy balance of nutritional foods to supplement and enhance their workouts.

Structuring Your Daily Nutrition Program

To receive the most benefit from the HIT workout program, athletes should replace an unhealthy diet with a daily nutrition plan that equals the exact number of calories that their activity levels require. On average, a female weighing 130 pounds requires a minimum of 1,747 calories daily and a male at 170 pounds requires a minimum of 2,276 calories daily. These figures do not include calories burned during training.

To determine the percentages of calories in a daily eating plan, add the complex carbohydrates, fat, and protein. It takes 2,500 calories to create a pound of muscle. Calculate the total number of calories burned in a given day and then add 350 calories if the goal is to build one pound of muscle in a week (350 × 7 = 2,450). Athletes who want to lose weight need to burn 3,500 calories per week to lose one pound of fat. Evaluate what the average nutrition day looks like and expand the daily nutrition plan to address pre- and posttraining fuel, rehydration, and muscle and liver glycogen storage. Then, schedule four to six balanced small meals daily for one week and keep a journal of the effects on training and competition. Modify evening eating to eliminate late-night junk food snacking, and commit to eating properly 90 percent of the time.

SUPPLEMENTS:
THE WHAT, WHY, WHO, AND WHEN

There is an unlimited market in the United States for a quick fix in muscle building, aerobic endurance, increased energy, and fat burning. The quick fix comes in many forms: pills, capsules, magical power bars, exotic creams, sprays, and drinks. Americans are bombarded by mass media campaigns that all have a common underlying theme: "If you take this supplement, you will magically get bigger, faster, stronger, and leaner, and the results will immediately gratify your needs!"

The supplement market exploded in 1994 when the FDA passed the Dietary Supplement Health and Education act (DSHEA), which defined supplements as "basically any vitamin, mineral, herb, or other botanicals, amino acids, any dietary substance for use by man to supplement the diet by increasing the total dietary intake." Supplements are readily available anywhere, anytime, anyplace, with no purchasing restrictions or limitations.

It is common to find supplement products being marketed or endorsed by successful athletes to imply that the supplement will dramatically improve performance. These athletes' world-class performances are probably based on superior genetics and hard work rather than the magical supplement. The FDA basically opened up the door for the sale of any snake oil supplement, regardless of the outrageous health and fitness claim, as long as the supplement is not being sold as a drug to treat or cure a disease.

There are no federal requirements or guidelines for purity, quality, or dosage when it comes to supplement sales. When the Centers for Science in Public Interest evaluated the quality and purity of randomly purchased supplements in the greater Washington, D.C., metro area, they found that 65 percent of the products they submitted to an independent laboratory for analysis were mislabeled—what was on the label was not in the bottle! To ensure quality control, savvy consumers can check each supplement's label to be sure it has the United States Pharmacopeia (USP) seal on the back panel. At least supplements with the USP code contain what the label says they do. But just what will the supplement do for an athlete's performance? Following are three of the supplements that the athletic population currently seems most drawn to.

Ma huang (ephedrine). Marketed as a metabolism booster, ephedrine has been linked to adverse health effects in healthy young adults without known risk factors. These adverse health effects include dizziness, abnormal heart rhythm, seizure, stroke, heart attack, psychosis, and death when using more than 25 milligrams. Herbal Fen-Fen from NutriSystem, for example, has used 40 milligrams of ephedrine per dose in its weight loss supplement. It is frequently marketed in combination with other drugs and is the most powerful of the "magical stack of three." Often this stack consists of 5 to 15 milligrams of ephedrine, 150 milligrams of caffeine, and 330 milligrams of aspirin.

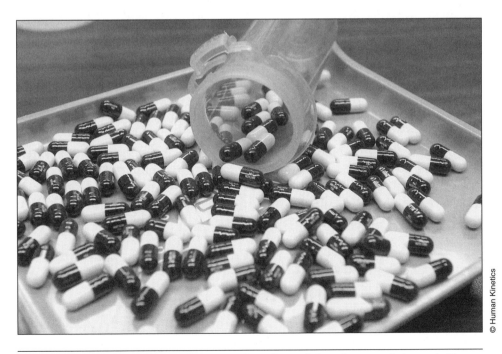

© Human Kinetics

Some athletes use supplements that are supposed to enhance their performance, but many bottles are mislabeled, and most supplements have dangerous risks and side effects.

Creatine phosphate. This substance is an amino acid that directly helps restore ATP and helps reduce lactic acid accumulation during intense exercise—that is, MMF. Creatine phosphate is found naturally stored in the body's muscles with one to two grams of daily intake from food. The body makes creatine in the liver, pancreas, and kidneys. It appears that taking creatine supplements may increase stored creatine by as much as 40 percent for young, highly trained athletes engaged in explosive endeavors. Neither the loading phase of this product, which consists of 20 grams the first week, nor the ongoing dose of 5 grams per day is recommended. In fact, it is preferable for athletes to eat a balanced diet and get these amino acids naturally from any protein source or combination of protein sources that have all nine essential amino acids. However, if an athlete is involved with a sport that is absolutely based on explosive power and speed or dependent on ATP-CP, then supplementing 1 to 2 grams daily may improve performance. Athletes sometimes overdose with this supplement, thinking that more is better. Overdosing will most likely produce negative side effects such as dehydration and cramping. In addition, it will depress the athlete's ability to produce the 1 to 2 grams normally produced naturally each day.

Androstenedione (andro). Andro is just the next step up from DHEA (dehydroepiandrosterone) and is the direct precursor to testosterone. Taken orally, andro is converted to testosterone in the liver. This supplement comes from the pollen of the Scotch pine tree. The concern for supplementing with any testosterone precursor is that the body's own internal production of testosterone may be depressed, and, depending on the duration and degree of supplement dosage, the general side effects associated with anabolic steroids—heart disease, liver cancer, depression, hostility, aggression, eating disorders, beard growth, acne, and masculinization and feminization—are all of great concern.

DHEA and andro are both testosterone precursors that an athlete's body will readily convert to increased testosterone levels. However, the body will often overcompensate with increased estrogen levels, and this is just one of the many concerns when considering supplementation.

The general recommendation for athletes supplementing is to establish a balanced daily eating plan as described earlier in this chapter and then consult a sports nutritionist or dietitian.

SOUND SLEEP WITHOUT INTERRUPTION

Athletes eat and sleep similarly to nonathletic people, yet they expect to have unlimited energy and power during every training session, especially during competition. Getting eight to nine hours of restful sleep seven days per week is essential for maximizing growth hormone response and utilization. The nocturnal release of growth hormone (GH) peaks after approximately one to two hours of sleep and then gradually tapers off during the next seven to eight hours of sleep. To maximize athletic cellular repair, it is better to err on the side of more sleep rather than less. Often athletes have trouble falling asleep, making it difficult to get six to seven hours of sleep. Coaches and parents need to work with athletes to identify the underlying causes of the disturbances, such as dehydration, excessive late nights, overtraining, excessive television or video games, or relationship problems.

Success of the HIT strength training system relies on the athlete's ability to train at 100 percent during every strength session. The athlete is like a fine tuned racecar that needs to be running on all cylinders with high-octane fuel and optimal maintenance. This means that athletes must always strive for good nutrition, adequate hydration, appropriate use of supplements, and plenty of sleep. It's important to expand training to include the often-overlooked areas of nutrition, hydration with electrolytes, sleep, and flexibility.

CHAPTER

Structuring a HIT Workout

There are literally hundreds of ways to create a strength training program, but the HIT system makes it easy for athletes to create personalized strength training programs that are both time efficient and effective. These HIT-based programs are not designed to build competitive weightlifters or bodybuilders; instead, they're focused on building maximum athletic strength to reduce injuries and improve power, speed, and agility.

The goal of this chapter is to describe the variables and options, or "tools," available for designing a HIT workout routine. These options include the following:

▸ Varied exercise modalities (that is, equipment) and resistance applications designed to shock the neuromuscular system, such as free weights, dumbbells, machines, cables, free motion devices, and manuals

▸ Advanced overload training (AOT) for maximal muscle fiber recruitment

▸ Varied split routines for the upper and lower body and variations in both the exercises used and the order in which the major muscle groups are worked

▸ Isolation and multijoint movements (pre- and postexhaustion scenarios)

▸ Varied rep ranges and recovery times between sets

The body adapts quickly to repeated stimuli and needs to be challenged constantly through such measures as changing the order in which the major muscle groups are trained, varying the selection of exercises, and choosing different angles of resistance. These program variations, which

are the foundation of the HIT system, create both psychological and neuromuscular stimulation, shocking the system so that the muscles and mind never become bored. Many traditional programs perform the same exercises in the same order whenever certain body parts are trained, leading to neurological staleness and eventual muscle imbalance. HIT workout programs focus on six to eight different upper body routines, using 12 to 16 exercises, and six to eight different lower body routines, again using 12 to 16 exercises. HIT programs vary the order of body parts, alternate push and pull body parts, use different modalities, employ different pre- and postexhaustion scenarios, alter the number of sets per exercise, use different rep ranges, and incorporate different types of AOT.

When designing strength workouts, you must take into account the available equipment, which, in many cases, may be limited or in poor working condition. Such situations will undoubtedly make it challenging to vary routines. On the other hand, some athletes and coaches may be fortunate enough to train in a facility with numerous exercise selections and the opportunity to design a great deal of variety in the strength routines. Consequently, the facility and its resources can greatly influence the design of strength training programs—but it should never prevent an athlete from having a successful training program. Regardless of the availability of varied exercise modalities, athletes who train consistently and put forth the effort to push to MMF can always get stronger (see table 7.1).

Some believe that free weights should be used exclusively to build strength, size, power, and balance; however, they are no more effective than other strength training modalities. The bottom line is that muscles don't know what type of modality is being used to apply the resistance. Whether it is free weights, machines, cables, or manual resistance, the muscles simply perceive the stimulus as resistance. Furthermore, muscles respond most favorably to neurological variety and, for optimum strength

Table 7.1 Training Scenarios

Less-than-ideal	Ideal
1978 Universal multistation gym 1979 Leg curl and extension	Complete iso lateral Hammer/Nautilus-Nitro/ Cybex/full dumbbell racks and Olympic benches
Minimum budget for equipment	Generous budget for equipment
Dated design (older equipment)	State-of-the-art equipment
Broken or malfunctioning equipment	Well-maintained equipment
Minimal space (800-1,000 sq. ft.)	Plenty of space
Limited exercise choices: free weights and Universal multistation gym	Many choices and numerous programs

Whether the gym available to an athlete is limited or ample, athletes can find a way to vary their workouts and implement the HIT strength system.

gains, athletes should try to use as many types of training modalities as possible. Regardless of the type of resistance to be used, designing a strength workout begins with selecting a specific number of exercises and placing them in a specific order on the workout card. Let's begin by designing a basic workout for the upper body.

UPPER BODY WORKOUTS

In designing an upper body workout, the goal should be to produce completely balanced muscles throughout the upper body and to focus on those areas that, when neglected, can lead to increased risk of injury. Athletes should incorporate exercises for the neck and rotator cuff and should be conscious of scapula movements during all upper body exercises.

Four-way neck exercises are beneficial for any athlete, especially for those involved in contact sports. Strengthening the neck in all four directions—flexion, extension, lateral right, and lateral left—helps to protect the spine and head from serious injury. The four-way neck movements should be performed first, executing 10 to 12 perfect reps to MMF for each movement followed by an isolation shrug movement. The exception is when training a large group of athletes with a limited number of neck machines. In this case, the athletes have to incorporate manual resistance with a partner (see manuals in chapter 11).

Scapula movements are incorporated into all upper body push and pull movements; the athlete should be especially conscious of these movements while performing multijoint exercises. While moving through the reps, the athlete may choose to isometrically stabilize the scapula in a neutral position or perform any one of the following four scapula movements during each rep: adduction, abduction, elevation, and depression.

Many strength programs have a tendency to neglect certain exercises that are critical to the integrity of the shoulder girdle. Among these often-neglected exercises are the single-joint isolation movements for the external and internal rotator cuff muscles. The NSPA medical experts believe that the external rotators (the infraspinatus and teres minor) and the internal rotators (the pecs, lats, teres major, and subscapularis) need to be integrated into the upper body workouts to help avoid injuries. Incorporating both the external and internal rotators helps balance the integrity of the shoulder joint. These exercises can be done with machines, tubes, bands, or manuals.

Multijoint Push and Pull Movements

A multijoint upper body movement is an exercise that uses two or more joints to perform the action—for example, using the shoulder and elbow to perform a seated press. This type of exercise is also referred to as a dual-joint or compound movement, and it has a straight, linear direction. Multijoint "push" exercises primarily involve the anterior muscle groups, including the pectorals, medial deltoids, and anterior deltoids. Multijoint "pull" exercises primarily involve the posterior muscle groups, including the latissimus dorsi, posterior deltoids, rhomboids, and traps. The biceps are also trained during the pull exercises, and all multijoint upper body movements involve the triceps. All multijoint movements involve more muscles than isolation movements do, which is why advanced overload multiple sets are most often performed with multijoint movements. The effort increases as more muscles are involved.

There are five distinct angles for all multijoint push movements, and these angles are separated by 45 degrees within a 0- to 180-degree range. These include dips (0 degrees), the decline press (45 degrees), the chest press (90 degrees), the incline press (135 degrees), and the seated press (180 degrees). There are also five distinct angles of movement for all pull movements, and these are also separated by 45 degrees within a 0- to 180-degree range. The pull movements include the vertical row (0 degrees), the low row (45 degrees), the seated row (90 degrees), the high row (135 degrees), and the lat pulldown (180 degrees). Table 7.2 illustrates all five multijoint (M) upper body push and pull movements in the five distinct angles of movement. In addition, the table describes the primary targeted muscles for each movement. Notice the direct opposite, or antagonistic, movements for each distinct angle of push and pull.

Table 7.2 Multijoint Upper Body Movements

Push movements prime movers	Pull movements prime movers
Seated press: 0° medial and anterior deltoids, triceps	Pulldown: 0° latissimus dorsi, teres major, biceps
Incline press: 45° anterior and medial deltoids, triceps	High row: 45° latissimus dorsi, teres major, rhomboids, biceps
Chest press: 90° pectoralis minor and major, anterior deltoids, triceps	Horizontal row: 90° posterior deltoids, latissimus dorsi, rhomboids, biceps
Decline press: 135° pectoralis minor and major, triceps	Low row: 135° posterior deltoids, latissimus dorsi, mid- and upper trapezius, biceps
Dip: 180° pectoralis major and minor, triceps	Vertical row: 180° posterior deltoids, upper trapezius, biceps

To create balance when designing the upper body strength program, there must be an equal number of push and pull exercises per workout. Each workout should include two to three distinct multijoint push movements and two to three distinct multijoint pull movements. Since there are five distinct multijoint movements for both push and pull exercises, NSPA recommends incorporating all five angles into five to six different upper body routines.

Single-Joint Push and Pull Movements

A single-joint upper body movement is performed through the action of only one joint and is commonly referred to as an *isolation movement*. A majority of single-joint movements are angular in nature and have a rotary strength curve. Single-joint "push" exercises, such as those working the pectoral muscles, anterior deltoids, and medial deltoids, primarily isolate the anterior muscle groups. The single-joint "pull" exercises, such as those working the latissimus dorsi, posterior deltoids, rhomboids, and teres major, primarily isolate the posterior muscle groups. Single-joint exercises can isolate larger muscle groups of the upper body and are not limited by the triceps or biceps reaching MMF before fatigue has occurred in the larger muscles. Most machines today have built-in cams or use levers to apply direct variable resistance throughout the entire angular strength curve. Dumbbells are affected by gravity and do not allow for any type of strength curve adjustment during single-joint movements, so athletes must take advantage of biomechanical angles and manual resistance to compensate for the lack of direct rotary resistance through the strength curve.

Single-joint exercises isolate the larger muscles of the body, allowing athletes to achieve 100 percent MMF. For example, during the free-weight bench press, the pectorals are not taken to complete MMF because the smaller triceps and anterior deltoid muscles fatigue first and cause the movement to stop. To bring the chest muscles to complete failure, the free-weight bench press may be followed by the chest cross isolation, which does not involve the triceps and shoulders, allowing for pectoral MMF. Thus, the key role of isolation movements is to enable the large, core muscles to reach maximum strength. Single-joint exercises can be placed before a multijoint exercise that works the same muscle group to set up a preexhaustion scenario, or single-joint exercises can be placed after a multijoint exercise that works the same muscle group to set up a postexhaustion scenario. Single-joint movements are challenging to spot because of the unique angular strength curve involved, especially when dumbbells are used (see "The Art of Spotting" in chapter 10).

Table 7.3 lists all the single-joint upper body push and pull exercises and shows the primary muscle involved in each movement.

Many athletes have been told that they must work the largest muscle groups first. Of course, this is true to some degree, and all the major muscle groups should have the opportunity to be worked first. A majority of the male population will always work the pecs first, but it's better to vary the order of the major muscle groups. The HIT system recognizes that all

Table 7.3 Single-Joint Upper Body Movements

Push movements prime movers	Pull movements prime movers
Iso lateral raise medial deltoids	Iso lat vertical push-down latissimus dorsi
Iso frontal raise/incline chest cross anterior deltoids	Iso lat pullover/iso lat pulldown latissimus dorsi
Iso chest cross pectoralis major and minor	Iso post delt row posterior deltoids, latissimus dorsi, mid- and upper trapezius
Iso decline chest cross pectoralis major and minor	Iso decline row posterior deltoids, latissimus dorsi, mid- and upper trapezius
Iso depression pectoralis major and minor	Iso shrug upper trapezius
Biceps flexion biceps	Triceps extension triceps
Wrist flexion forearm flexors	Wrist extension forearm extensors

upper body core muscle groups are equal. These muscle groups should be trained in varying orders to avoid focusing on one muscle group more than another and creating muscle group imbalance. Use the opposing push and pull muscle sets in table 7.4 to prevent this imbalance. Training is not about moving from the largest to the smallest muscle groups; it is about creating muscular balance throughout the upper body.

HIT designs upper body workouts that incorporate a minimum of six major muscle groups (three push and three pull), plus biceps and triceps.

The upper body routines in table 7.5 illustrate ways to vary the order of major muscle groups and alternate push and pull muscle groups. The biceps and triceps are always worked last so that they are not preexhausted; after

Table 7.4 Opposing Muscle Sets

Push	Pull
Pectorals	Latissimus dorsi
Anterior delts	Posterior delts
Medial delts	Traps
Triceps	Biceps

Table 7.5 Upper Body Routines

Option 1	Option 2	Option 3	Option 4
Pectorals (push)	Latissimus dorsi (pull)	Medial deltoids (push)	Posterior deltoids (pull)
Latissimus dorsi (pull)	Anterior deltoids (push)	Trapezius (pull)	Pectorals (push)
Medial deltoids (push)	Posterior deltoids (pull)	Anterior deltoids (push)	Latissimus dorsi (pull)
Posterior deltoids (pull)	Medial deltoids (push)	Posterior deltoids (pull)	Medial deltoids (push)
Anterior deltoids (push)	Trapezius (pull)	Pectorals (push)	Trapezius (pull)
Trapezius (pull)	Pectorals (push)	Latissimus dorsi (pull)	Anterior deltoids (push)
Triceps (push)	Biceps (pull)	Triceps (push)	Biceps (pull)
Biceps (pull)	Triceps (push)	Biceps (pull)	Triceps (push)

three multijoint push movements, the triceps will experience three sets of MMF unless the major muscle was preexhausted. These routines do not include four-way neck exercises or abdominals. The template routine consists of one multijoint and one single-joint exercise for each major muscle group, with the exception of biceps and triceps, so that the total number of exercises and sets is 14.

Now that you're aware of the many variables to consider when putting together an upper body strength workout, the next task is to choose exercises for each major muscle group. A basic template is created for the upper body strength training program by selecting two exercises, one multijoint and one single joint, for each major muscle group. These should include the following:

- One multijoint chest exercise (e.g., bench) and one single-joint chest exercise (pec fly)
- One multijoint lat exercise (pull-up) and one single-joint lat exercise (pullover)
- One multijoint medial deltoid exercise (seated press) and one single-joint medial deltoid exercise (lateral raise)
- One multijoint posterior deltoid exercise (seated row) and one single-joint posterior deltoid exercise (iso row)
- One multijoint incline press (incline bench) and one single-joint exercise for the chest and anterior deltoids (frontal raise)
- One multijoint incline row and one single-joint lat exercise (cable high row)
- One biceps exercise and one triceps exercise (dumbbell curls and cable triceps)

Total number of exercises = 14.

This routine represents a basic template and will have numerous variations as you design additional routines.

Table 7.6 shows the numerous choices you have when designing a workout routine for the upper body. If the last major muscle group worked is a pull muscle group, the triceps should follow. If the last major muscle group worked is a push muscle group, biceps should follow.

When a single-joint, isolation exercise is performed before a multijoint exercise and targets the same muscle group, it is considered a preexhaustion scenario: The primary core muscle is taken to MMF. An athlete who wants to perform an advanced overload technique (AOT) should recover for 5 to 30 seconds and then perform the multijoint movement for the same muscle group to MMF. With this brief recovery, the primary muscle will replenish less than 50 percent of its ATP-CP and will reach failure before the triceps and/or biceps. This allows for deeper muscle tissue breakdown.

Table 7.6 Workout Routine Choices for the Upper Body

Muscle groups (push/pull)	Multijoint (compound)	Single-joint (isolation)
Pectorals, anterior deltoids (push)	Chest press: free weight, dumbbell, machine, cable, Smith, push-up, manual	Iso chest cross: machine chest cross or pec fly, dumbbell fly, cable cross, manual
Latissimus dorsi, posterior deltoids (pull)	Lat pulldown: chin-up/pull-up, machine pulldown, manual	Iso lat: machine pullover, cable lat pulldown, manual
Medial deltoids, pectorals, anterior deltoids (push)	Seated press: machine, free weight, dumbbell, Smith, cable, manual	Iso lateral raise: machine lateral raise, cable, dumbbell, manual
Posterior deltoids, latissimus dorsi (pull)	Seated row: free weight, machine, cable row, T-bar row, dumbbell, manual	Iso rear delt row: machine isolation row, dumbbell, cable, manual
Anterior deltoids (push)	Incline press: machine, free weight, dumbbell, Smith, cable, push-up, manual	Iso frontal raise: machine frontal raise, cable, dumbbell, manual
Latissimus dorsi, posterior deltoids (pull)	High row: machine, cable, manual	Iso high row: machine, cable, manual
Anterior deltoids, pectorals (push)	Decline and dip press: machine, chair, manual	Iso depression: machine, cable, manual
Trapezius, posterior deltoids (pull)	Vertical and low row: cable, dumbbell, manual	Iso shrug: cable, Smith, free weight, machine, dumbbell, manual

Some examples include performing the chest fly followed by the chest press or performing the lat pullover followed by the lat pulldown. Keep in mind that less recovery directly affects the amount of weight used when performing a multijoint movement. Another option is to recover 75 to 90 seconds between the single-joint and multijoint movements, but to keep in mind that the major muscles will recover and the weakest link, the triceps and biceps, will fail first.

When a single-joint exercise is performed after a multijoint exercise and targets the same muscle group, it is considered a postexhaustion scenario. An example is the chest press followed by the chest fly, or the lat pulldown followed by the lat pullover. The triceps and biceps are not used during single-joint movements, allowing the primary muscle to go to complete failure. The amount of recovery will dictate the amount of weight used during the single-joint isolation movement.

Table 7.7 presents three separate upper body workouts using the single-set protocol and pre- and postexhaustion scenarios.

There is little research showing that using preexhaustion techniques when training is more effective than using postexhaustion techniques. Some athletes prefer one to the other. NSPA recommends using both to shock the neuromuscular system and create variety.

Table 7.8 presents three different upper body workouts, with a total of 14 sets for each workout. These routines offer variety to create greater stimulus and, therefore, greater strength gains.

The one-set routine is made up of 14 different exercises; it includes one set per exercise, and each major muscle group is trained using a postexhaustion scenario. The two-set routine is made up of eight different exercises, six of which are multijoint movements, and includes two sets per exercise. There are only two isolation movements in this routine: one for the biceps and one for the triceps. The three-set routine is made up of six different exercises, four of which are multijoint movements, and includes three sets per exercise. The biceps or triceps will reach MMF six times apiece while performing the multijoint movements. The isolation of the biceps and triceps at the end of this routine is optional, considering the

Table 7.7 Three Options for Upper Body Workouts

Muscle group	Preexhaustion upper body routine (option 1)	Postexhaustion upper body routine (option 2)	Mixed pre and post upper body routine (option 3)
Pectorals	Cable chest cross (S) Dumbbell bench press (M)	Free bench press (M) Machine chest cross (S)	Machine chest press (M) Dumbbell fly (S)
Latissimus dorsi	Machine pullover (S) Pull-up (M)	Machine pulldown (M) Machine pullover (S)	Decline dumbbell pullover (S) Chin-up (M)
Medial deltoids	Machine lateral raise (S) Dumbbell seated press (M)	Machine seated press (M) Dumbbell lateral raise (S)	Cable lateral raise (S) Machine seated press (M)
Posterior deltoids	Rear delt iso row (S) Machine seated row (M)	T-bar row (M) Manual iso row (S)	Rear delt iso row (S) Dumbbell bent-over row (S)
Anterior deltoids	Cable frontal raise (S) Free incline press (M)	Dumbbell incline press (M) Dumbbell frontal raise (S)	Machine incline press (M) Manual frontal raise (S)
Trapezius	Dumbbell shrug (S)	Machine shrug (S)	Manual shrug (S)
Triceps	Cable (S)	Machine (S)	Manual (S)
Biceps	Machine (S)	Dumbbell (S)	Curl bar (S)

(S) = Single-joint exercise; (M) = Multijoint exercise

Table 7.8 Upper Body Workout Routines

1-Set routine (14 exercises, 14 sets)	2-Set routine (8 exercises, 14 sets)	3-Set routine (6 exercises, 14 sets)
Lat pulldown (M)	Lat pulldown (M)	Lat pulldown (M)
Lat pullover (S)	Lat pulldown (M)	Lat pulldown (M)
Chest press (M)	Chest press (M)	Lat pulldown (M)
Chest cross (S)	Chest press (M)	Chest press (M)
Seated row (M)	Seated row (M)	Chest press (M)
Iso seated row (S)	Seated row (M)	Chest press (M)
Seated press (M)	Seated press (M)	Seated row (M)
Lateral raise (S)	Seated press (M)	Seated row (M)
Incline row (M)	Low row (M)	Seated row (M)
Iso incline row (S)	Low row (M)	Seated press (M)
Incline press (M)	Incline press (M)	Seated press (M)
Incline cross (S)	Incline press (M)	Seated press (M)
Biceps curl (S)	Biceps curl (S)	Biceps curl (S)
Triceps extension (S)	Triceps extension (S)	Triceps extension (S)

(S) = Single-joint exercise; (M) = Multijoint exercise

number of sets these muscles will already have performed to MMF. As you can see, the HIT program gives you the opportunity to create numerous programs that add beneficial variety to the workout.

Optional Combinations for Upper Body Shocking

Optional combinations add variety to a strength training routine. They involve multiple sets with different multijoint and single-joint combinations focusing on the same muscle group (see table 7.9 for one example). Recovery times between sets can also be manipulated to increase the difficulty level.

LOWER BODY WORKOUTS

Lower body workouts are much simpler to design than upper body workouts because there are fewer total muscle groups and exercise selections and, in many cases, fewer equipment options. Lower body exercises have

Table 7.9 Optional Routines for Chest

Routine options	Set 1	Set 2	Set 3
One	Fr. bench (M)	Chest cross (S)	
Two	DB fly (S)	DB bench (M)	
Three	H. bench (M)	H. bench (M)	H. bench (M)
Four	Fr. bench (M)	Manual fly (S)	Fr. bench (M)
Five	Cable fly (S)	DB bench (M)	Cable fly (S)
Six	DB bench (M)	H. bench (M)	Fr. bench (M)

DB = Dumbbell; Fr. = Free weight; H. = Hammer

some unique characteristics that should be mentioned. For example, the majority of hip and leg exercises are single-joint movements, but those that are multijoint movements involve the hip joint and knee joint. Also, every time multijoint hip exercises are performed, both push and pull muscle groups work simultaneously, and some more than others—for example, the quadriceps, hamstrings, and gluteus all work when performing the leg press. Because training the lower body often involves heavier weight and includes movement that involves the lower back, athletes should always strive to perform these exercises with perfect execution and form. Exercises of particular concern are free-weight squats, deadlifts, and stiff-leg deadlifts. Table 7.10 breaks down the multijoint and single-joint exercises involving the hips, legs, and lower back.

Table 7.10 Lower Body Exercises

Push movements: prime movers	Pull movements: prime movers
Leg press/squat/lunge/(M) combination push and pull gluteus maximus, quadriceps, hamstrings	Lunge/leg press/squat/(M) combination push and pull hamstrings, quadriceps, gluteus maximus
Iso hip extension (S) gluteus maximus, hamstrings	Iso hip flexion (S) iliopsoas, rectus femoris
Iso hip abduction (S) gluteus medius and minimus, tensor fascia latae	Iso hip adduction (S) adductor magnus, longus, brevis gracilis, pectineus
Iso leg extension (S) vastus: lateralis, medialis, intermedius rectus femoris	Iso leg flexion (S) biceps femoris, tendinosis, semimembranosis
Iso ankle extension (S) gastrocnemius, soleus	Iso ankle flexion (S) tibialis anterior, extensor halligus longus

(S) = Single-joint exercise; (M) = Multijoint exercise

The following lower body exercises include secondary, antagonistic muscle groups that contract as stabilizers during multijoint exercises.

Multijoint

- ▶ Squat: free weight, sissy, front, Smith, dumbbell
- ▶ Leg press: Hammer, Nautilus, Cybex, hack squat machine
- ▶ Lunge: six-inch step dumbbell lunge, lunge-walk, Smith lunge
- ▶ Deadlift: Free weight, Smith, dumbbell

Single-joint

- ▶ Leg curl and leg extension
- ▶ Hip flexion and hip extension
- ▶ Hip adduction and hip abduction
- ▶ Stiff-leg deadlift
- ▶ Seated soleus raise, standing gastroc raise, and tibialis anterior

Similar to upper body workouts, lower body routines can be made up of many combinations of pre- and postexhaustion scenarios, especially since most lower body isolation movements have some impact on all lower body multijoint movements. In this sample preexhaustion scenario for the lower body, all single-joint exercises are followed by multijoint exercises: the Nautilus leg curl followed by the Hammer leg press, then leg extension followed by a free squat, and finally a manual hip extension followed by the Nautilus leg press.

This sample lower body postexhaustion scenario uses multijoint exercises followed by single-joint exercises: the Nautilus leg press followed by the Hammer leg extension, followed by a dumbbell lunge and Hammer hip extension, and finally sissy squats and the Nautilus leg curl.

Lower body workouts are less complicated than upper body workouts and most often do not require more than one piece of equipment for each exercise, with the exception of leg presses. Because some facilities lack the budget to have isolation leg machines, NSPA highly recommends learning how to perform manual resistance (see chapter 11). The benefits of using manuals in place of machines are full range of motion for each exercise, unlimited variations in angles of force, and the ability to implement with large groups.

The number of sets for an average lower body workout is 14 to 16. This includes the lower back extension. As a guideline, it's best to start with a multijoint exercise to warm up both the hip and the knee joints. When performing multiple sets, perform primarily hip movements, leg presses, deadlifts, leg extensions, and leg curls, because these exercises require greater muscular involvement. Tables 7.11 and 7.12 show exercise selections that can be used in a lower body workout.

Table 7.11 Lower Body Workout Samples

Workout 1 12 exercises, 12 sets	Workout 2 12 exercises, 14 sets	Workout 3 10 exercises, 15 sets	Workout 4 8 exercises, 16 sets
Leg press A (M)	Leg press A (M)	Leg press B (M)	Leg extension (S)
Leg extension (S)	Leg press A (M)	Leg press A (M)	Leg extension (S)
Leg curl (S)	Leg curl (S)	Leg press A (M)	Leg press A (M)
Lunge (M)	Leg curl (S)	Hip extensor (S)	Leg curl (S)
Deadlift (M)	Leg extension (S)	Hip adductor (S)	Leg press A (M)
Hip extensor (S)	Leg extension (S)	Leg extension (S)	Leg curl (S)
Back extension (S)	Stiff-leg deadlift (S)	Leg extension (S)	Leg press A (M)
Hip abductor (S)	Deadlift (M)	Leg press B (M)	Hip extensor (S)
Hip adductor (S)	Hip adductor (S)	Back extension (S)	Hip extensor (S)
Hip flexor (S)	Hip extensor (S)	Back extension (S)	Hip flexor (S)
Ankle flexion (S)	Hip abductor (S)	Hip flexor (S)	Hip flexor (S)
Ankle extension (S)	Leg press B (M)	Hip abductor (S)	Deadlift (M)
	Ankle extension (S)	Deadlift (M)	Deadlift (M)
	Ankle flexion (S)	Deadlift (M)	Deadlift (M)
		Ankle flexion (S)	Back extension (S)
			Ankle extension (S)

Leg press A = Nautilus leg press; Leg press B = Hammer leg press; (S) = Single-joint exercise; (M) = Multijoint exercise

LARGE GROUP PROGRAMMING

NSPA has designed strength programs for dozens of high schools with limited equipment and time. Let's take a team with 40 players who have 45 minutes to work out, four times a week. Half the athletes may work on the upper body while the other half works on the lower body. Each group is split into pairs so that there are 10 pairs training the upper body and 10 pairs training the lower body. The coach designs 10 separate routines for both the upper and lower body, with each pair of athletes starting with a different exercise. Utilizing every piece of equipment available and incorporating manuals in some routines also help. Each routine will include 12 to 14 sets, and some exercises may use multiple sets. If the 10 routines are designed properly, there should never be two pairs at one

Table 7.12 Lower Body Exercise Selections

Option 1	Option 2	Option 3
Hammer leg press (M)	Leg press (M)	Free squat (M)
Hammer leg press (M)	Leg press (M)	Free squat (M)
Hammer leg press (M)	Leg curl (S)	Free squat (M)
Leg extension (S)	Leg curl (S)	Hip extension (S)
Leg curl (S)	Leg extension (S)	Hip extension (S)
Hip extension (S)	Leg extension (S)	Hip extension (S)
Hip flexion (S)	Hip adduction (S)	Deadlift (M)
Deadlift (M)	Hip abduction (S)	Deadlift (M)
Deadlift (M)	Leg press (M)	Deadlift (M)
Deadlift (M)	Hip extension (S)	Leg curl (S)
Hip adduction (S)	Hip flexion (S)	Leg curl (S)
Hip abduction (S)	Deadlift (M)	Leg extension (S)
Back extension (S)	Stiff-leg deadlift (S)	Leg extension (S)
Soleus raise (S)	Gastro raise (S)	Back extension (S)
Shin curl (S)	Shin curl (S)	Toe raise (S)
Gastro raise (S)	Soleus raise (S)	Shin curl (S)

(S) = Single-joint exercise; (M) = Multijoint exercise

exercise. The coach may also use a whistle when it is time to move to the next exercise or time to perform the next set. The lower body programs are designed the same way. Each workout should have 12 to 14 sets. The time between the first and second athletes performing a set with a particular exercise should be no more than 15 seconds, and recovery time for each pair between exercises should be no more than 45 seconds. The total time for a pair of athletes to complete one set would be 3 minutes multiplied by 14 sets, or 42 minutes total.

The coach will have to keep the athletes on a timer and blow the whistle for each exercise transition. The athletes become very disciplined and focused on the job at hand and do not have time to socialize. It will take a few sessions for the athletes to get their exact weights and to get a feel for the times, but once they do, the circuit is an exciting and disciplined environment.

TRADITIONAL PROGRAMMING FLAWS

Many strength programs have been handed down from generation to generation unchanged, although historically they may be linked to recurring injuries because of the excessive volume in the program. Some of the traditional programming flaws include overuse of the rotator cuff and biceps, triceps, and pectoral muscles, as well as misjudging the appropriate number of exercises, sets, and weekly workouts.

The first programming error is overusing the rotator cuff. The traditional push and pull split is a common programming approach for the upper body but may lead to overuse injuries of the rotator cuff. For example, suppose that on Monday an athlete performs all push movements, including exercises for the chest, shoulders, and triceps, which involve the rotator cuff muscles—the supraspinatus, subscapularis, infraspinatus, and teres minor. On Tuesday, she performs all pull movements, including exercises for the back and biceps; these also involve the rotator cuff muscles. This upper body program will overtrain the rotator cuff muscles and is commonly associated with nagging shoulder pain or sharp pain felt during certain push movements, such as the free-weight bench press and overhead press. Unfortunately, many athletes are unaware of the pain's origin and continue to train hard, just hoping the pain will go away. The HIT system performs all upper body movements during the same lifting session so that smaller muscles such as the rotators are not overtrained.

Another traditional programming error is performing triceps or biceps exercises the day after a push or pull routine. An example of this is an athlete performing multijoint push movements on Monday and then isolation triceps on Tuesday, or performing pull multijoint movements on Wednesday and then isolation biceps on Thursday. This is considered a programming error because the triceps reach MMF first when performing any multijoint push movement, and the biceps reach MMF first when performing any multijoint pull movement, with the exception of a preexhaustion scenario. These muscle groups need a minimum of 48 hours of recovery time after performing multijoint movements to failure. When an athlete trains arms the day after performing multijoint push and pull movements, the strength potential is minimized and the risk for injury significantly increases.

Athletes must not overdo specific lifts, such as the free-weight bench press, because this will likely lead to muscle imbalances and injuries. The free-weight bench press is perhaps the most stressful exercise to the rotator cuff, and yet it is common for athletes to train the chest muscles three times per week using this exercise with multiple sets (6 to 8). In addition, some athletes poorly execute this lift and add AOT to every workout. The HIT system, instead, stresses perfect form and limits sets to a maximum of three sets for each muscle group. AOT is used only when there is a minimum of three days of recovery between workouts.

Many traditional strength programs incorporate different types of strength phases during the year, using pyramid sets, performing three to four exercises per body part, incorporating "light" days, and performing certain lifts that are ballistic in nature that could cause joint trauma. The HIT system is very simple; it builds strength to maximum levels and then maintains these strength gains throughout an entire athletic season. All sets are performed to MMF, all muscles are trained using only two to three sets or exercises per body part, and ballistic movements are never used.

Because there is a detailed science behind the HIT system and many different lifting options, it takes most coaches and athletes a few months to become familiar and comfortable with the program. Once athletes have mastered the HIT program, the task of designing effective workouts becomes a welcome challenge.

You are now able to design strength routines that incorporate balanced strength throughout the body. You know how to design a variety of upper and lower body routines with different programming variables, such as pre- and postexhaustion scenarios, different modalities, one- to three-set options, and a varied order of the major muscle groups. In addition, you should be able to recognize flaws with other, traditional programs and have the ability to correct those flaws to ensure strength balance between different muscle groups. In my experience, HIT athletes enjoy designing strength routines and discussing ways to create new ones.

CHAPTER

8

Developing Sport-Specific Programs

This chapter will focus on designing a sport-specific strength program based on energy system utilization, average duration of activity, recovery time between exercises, and functional power and strength assessment. These variables dictate the number of sets, rep range, time under tension, and recovery time between sets.

The body's primary energy source for all bodily functions, including muscle contractions, is a chemical compound known as adenosine triphosphate (ATP); however, only a small quantity of ATP is stored in the cell, and it must be continually resynthesized through chemical reactions—ATP to ADT and the metabolism of carbohydrates, fats, and proteins. The processes that yield ATP include the ATP-CP energy system, anaerobic glycolysis of carbohydrates, aerobic glycolysis of carbohydrates, and beta oxidation of fatty acids.

The factor that determines the primary energy source used during an activity is the level of intensity and the speed at which energy is needed to fuel the activity. Creatine phosphate (CP) is stored in the muscle tissue cells and readily available for the production of energy in the absence of oxygen; in fact, when the bond holding creatine and phosphate together is split through a chemical reaction, the energy release is almost instantaneous. Because of this quick process, the ATP-CP system is the primary source of energy during quick bursts of energy or when all-out effort is required; however, CP is stored in limited quantities and depletes in a short period of time—often in less than 10 seconds. If intensity remains high, another energy system, anaerobic glycolysis, must predominate to maintain the activity.

The process of anaerobic glycolysis, or the "cutting up" of carbohydrates, also occurs in the absence of oxygen and, therefore, is another quick source for yielding ATP. The by-product of anaerobic glycolysis, however, is the fatigue-causing lactic acid, and as fatigue sets in, intensity begins to drop. The energy system that predominates during the recovery period, aerobic glycolysis, metabolizes carbohydrates in the presence of oxygen to resynthesize ATP.

During aerobic glycolysis, the activity level is at an intensity where the body can clear away or use lactic acid for further energy production. It is also at this level that CP can be resynthesized and stored again for potential use through the ATP-CP energy system. Therefore, when performing intense activities such as weightlifting, recovery is vital to enable effective use of the anaerobic energy systems.

The final energy system, beta oxidation of fatty acids, yields the highest amount of ATP; however, it is a slow process and is used during those activities that are much lower in intensity or can be maintained for an extended period. In fact, this is the energy system that predominates while you are sleeping. Although proteins can be used in the aerobic production of ATP, they are not the preferred energy source and often not discussed in length when describing the energy systems. Instead, proteins are most often discussed in the context of tissue building and repair.

The energy systems function as a continuum, not like an on–off switch. Some athletes mistakenly think that the ATP-CP system shuts off after a certain number of seconds, when in fact the stores simply deplete and ATP-CP can no longer be the primary source to fuel the activity. Others believe that fat stores are only mobilized after a certain number of minutes, when in fact fat and carbohydrates are both always being used; the availability of oxygen and intensity determine the rate at which each is used.

In designing sport-specific strength programs, it is important to consider the predominant energy system used during the activity and then match it with the most compatible rep ranges and recovery time between sets. For example, I would not recommend that a marathoner who uses aerobic energy systems perform 4 to 6 reps to MMF with two to three minutes of recovery between sets or that a shot-putter who uses the ATP-CP energy system perform 16 to 20 reps to MMF with 30 to 60 seconds of recovery between sets.

Table 8.1 serves as a reference for athletes developing a strength training program for a specific sport. Keep in mind that this is not an exact science; many times it is necessary to rely on more information about a particular athlete's specific genetics, strengths, and limitations, as well as common sense, to determine the optimal strength training program. For instance, let's compare a golfer and shot-putter. Both sports require the ATP-CP anaerobic energy system, because the bouts of effort rely on acceleration and power and are brief, and both have five minutes or more of recovery between activities. In addition, both sports generate maximum speed—one into the head of the golf club and the other into

Table 8.1 General Guidelines for Energy System Utilization

Energy utilization/ sport	Activity duration	Recovery intervals	Rep range	Time under tension	Recovery between sets
Aerobic endurance marathon, triathlon	30 min. or more	None	15-20	90-120 sec.	30-60 sec.
Aerobic/anaerobic 1-mile run, golf*	5-15 min.	None	12-15	72-90 sec.	60-90 sec.
Anaerobic/repeat football, lacrosse, basketball, soccer	30-180 sec.	30-120 sec.	8-12	48-72 sec.	90-120 sec.
Anaerobic ATP-CP shot-putter, weightlifter	0-10 sec.	5 min. or more	4-8	24-48 sec.	2-3 min.

*Exception to rule

a 16-pound shot put. So it would appear that athletes who participate in these sports should both perform four to eight reps to MMF with two to three minutes of recovery between sets; however, as table 8.1 shows, it's recommended that these athletes work out differently. The table assumes that functional power and strength assessment is a key component of each athletic endeavor.

AEROBIC ENDURANCE SPORTS

Aerobic endurance sports, which have no recovery periods and last more than 30 minutes, include such activities as running marathons, participating in triathlons, swimming, cycling, rowing, cross-country skiing, and skating. The average heart rate during these activities is 65 to 80 percent of the athlete's calculated maximum heart rate (determined by subtracting age from 220). When training an endurance athlete, it's important not to aim for maximum explosive power or size, because these would only hinder the athlete's energy efficiency during competition. Instead, the endurance athlete should be trained for muscle endurance and stamina. In fact, on occasion, NSPA has found great success with this type of athlete by developing a program involving rep ranges of 25 or more reps with minimal, 30-second recovery and super-slow reps lasting 12 to 14 seconds each while reaching MMF in less than 120 seconds.

Endurance athletes have a primary energy system that uses beta oxidation of fatty acids. The endurance athlete's genetic profile includes varying degrees of ectomorph body type and a high percentage of slow-twitch, type I muscle fibers. The blood lactate levels are negligible because the primary energy system used is beta oxidation, whose by-product of metabolism is water and not lactic acid.

Specific strength training guidelines exist for aerobic endurance athletes who use the HIT program. The recommended rep range for athletes who participate in aerobic endurance sports is 15 to 20 reps to MMF; however, this type of athlete can also benefit from rep ranges up to 25 reps or more to push the muscle tissue into an extended MMF set for greater slow-twitch muscle fiber recruitment and fatigue.

Follow these strength training guidelines:

▶ Increase resistance 3 to 5 percent when 20 reps are reached or time under tension is greater than 120 seconds.

▶ Perform one set per exercise.

▶ Allow between 30 and 60 seconds of recovery between sets.

▶ Perform two upper body workouts per week, each totaling 6 to 8 sets of exercises, and two lower body workouts per week, each totaling 6 to 8 sets of exercises, or perform two full body workouts, each totaling 12 to 14 sets of exercises.

AOT is not typically used when training an endurance athlete, but it certainly could be of use if the athlete thinks it necessary to reach deeper into the muscle tissue for added strength and muscle hypertrophy.

The short recovery time between sets keeps the heart rate above 55 percent of the max HR and enhances aerobic conditioning. Some coaches mistakenly believe that strength training is not necessary for athletes who participate in endurance sports. This might be true if an endurance athlete spends excessive time in the weight room training like a bodybuilder and ends up with too much bulk, thus negatively affecting sport performance. But when an endurance athlete trains appropriately with the HIT program, the performance benefits can be enormous.

Many endurance athletes prefer the regular use of slow training protocols while performing sets—for example, six seconds positive and six seconds negative—because the technique requires less weight, thereby reducing joint stress. This is where time of tension comes into play: Although the total number of reps is reduced, the time of tension leading to MMF remains the same. This type of slow training has been proven to be just as effective as the HIT perfect rep speed of five to seven seconds, so both protocols may be used to create variety in the training program. Add optional biceps and triceps exercises for nine total exercises, and add optional hip adduction and abduction for 10 exercises. Also rotate straight and bent-leg calf raises. Tables 8.2 and 8.3 contain exercise routines for full, upper, and lower body workouts.

AEROBIC–ANAEROBIC SPORTS

Athletes who participate in sports that tap into both the aerobic and anaerobic energy systems require a consistent level of high energy output

Table 8.2 Full Body Workouts for Aerobic Endurance Athletes

Routine 1	Routine 2	Routine 3	Routine 4	Routine 5
Leg press	Chest press	Leg press	Dip	Shrug
Leg curl	Seated row	Leg curl	Chin-up	Chest press
Leg extension	Seated press	Leg extension	Seated press	Seated row
Hip extension	Pull-up	Hip extension	Seated row	Seated press
Hip flexion	Shrug	Hip flexion	Chest press	Pull-ups
Shin curl	Dip	Shin curl	Shrug	Dip
Toe raise	Leg press	Toe raise	Leg press	Leg press
Back extension	Leg extension	Back extension	Leg curl	Leg curl
Pull-up	Leg curl	Abdominals	Leg extension	Leg extension
Chest press	Hip extension	Seated row	Hip extension	Hip extension
Seated row	Hip flexion	Seated press	Hip flexion	Hip flexion
Seated press	Shin curl	Chin-up	Shin curl	Shin curl
Shrug	Toe raise	Chest press	Toe raise	Toe raise
Dip	Back extension	Shrug	Back extension	Back extension
Abdominals	Abdominals	Dip	Abdominals	Abdominals

when working at 80 to 90 percent of max HR for periods of 5 to 15 minutes without recovery. These athletes perform at an intensity that is on the edge of the anaerobic threshold, where lactic acid is being buffered with oxygen and their body is becoming more efficient at moving the lactic acid out of the muscles for energy production and excretion. Such training is especially important when athletes near the end of a competition and must reach even higher intensities, and deal with higher levels of lactic acid, in order to win. One common characteristic shared by aerobic–anaerobic athletes is that the primary energy system is an oxidative and glycolytic combination with high levels of lactic acid buffering. Other characteristics include participation in sports that require high levels of anaerobic conditioning and a genetic profile that is usually a combination of ectomorph and mesomorph body types. Most aerobic–anaerobic athletes also have an even mix of slow-twitch (type I) and fast twitch (type II) muscle fibers because of the combination of aerobic and anaerobic energy use.

The strength training guidelines for aerobic–anaerobic athletes differ from the guidelines for those who only participate in aerobic sports. The recommended rep range for athletes who participate in aerobic–anaerobic endurance sports is 12 to 15 reps to MMF; however, this type of athlete

Table 8.3   Upper and Lower Body Workouts for Aerobic Endurance Athletes

Upper body (7 sets, 7 exercises)				
Routine 1	**Routine 2**	**Routine 3**	**Routine 4**	**Routine 5**
Pull-up	Chest press	Seated row	Dip	Shrug
Chest press	Seated row	Seated press	Chin-up	Chest press
Seated row	Seated press	Chin-up	Seated press	Seated row
Seated press	Pull-up	Chest press	Seated row	Seated press
Shrug	Shrug	Shrug	Chest press	Pull-up
Dip	Dip	Dip	Shrug	Dip
Abdominals	Abdominals	Abdominals	Abdominals	Abdominals
Lower body (8 sets, 8 exercises)				
Routine 1	**Routine 2**	**Routine 3**	**Routine 4**	**Routine 5**
Leg press	Leg press	Leg press	Leg press	Leg press
Leg curl	Leg curl	Leg curl	Leg curl	Leg curl
Leg extension	Leg extension	Leg extension	Leg extension	Leg extension
Hip extension	Hip extension	Hip extension	Hip extension	Hip extension
Hip flexion	Hip flexion	Hip flexion	Hip flexion	Hip flexion
Toe raise	Toe raise	Toe raise	Toe raise	Toe raise
Shin curl	Shin curl	Shin curl	Shin curl	Shin curl
Back extension	Back extension	Back extension	Back extension	Back extension

can also benefit from rep ranges of 16 to 25 reps to push the muscle tissue into an extended MMF, as well as from occasionally lower rep ranges of 10 to 12 reps to develop greater power output.

Follow these strength training guidelines:

▶ Aim for a time-under-tension range of 72 to 100 seconds.

▶ Increase the weight by 3 to 5 percent when 15 reps are reached or the time under tension is greater than 100 seconds.

▶ Perform one set per exercise.

▶ Allow 60 to 75 seconds of recovery between sets.

▶ Perform two upper body workouts per week, each totaling 8 to 14 sets of exercises, and two lower body workouts per week, each totaling 8 to 14 sets of exercises, or perform two full body workouts per week, each totaling 14 to 20 sets of exercises.

▶ Allow AOT every three to four sessions.

▶ Follow the strength routines shown in tables 8.4 and 8.5.

ANAEROBIC SPORTS

Anaerobic sports require athletes to sustain high levels of energy output, with heart rate levels staying between 90 and 100 percent for periods of 30 seconds to three minutes, and to recover in a period ranging from approximately 30 seconds to 2 minutes. Recovery may be predetermined by the sport, such as with wrestling or boxing, or it may be unpredictable and based on the flow of the game, such as with football, soccer, lacrosse, basketball, tennis, and hockey. Therefore, anaerobic athletes benefit from

Table 8.4   Full Body Workouts for Aerobic–Anaerobic Sports*

Routine 1 18 exercises	Routine 2 18 exercises	Routine 3 16 exercises	Routine 4 15 exercises	Routine 5 15 exercises
Leg press	Chest press	Leg press	Dip	Shrug
Leg curl	Chest cross	Leg extension	Chin-up	Chest press
Leg extension	Seated row	Leg curl	Seated press	Seated row
Hip extension	Iso post delts	Hip flexion	Seated row	Seated press
Hip flexion	Seated press	Hip extension	Chest press	Pull-up
Shin curl	Frontal raise	Hip abduction	Shrug	Dip
Toe raise	Pull-up	Hip adduction	Leg press	Leg press
Back extension	Shrug	Back extension	Leg curl	Leg curl
Pull-up	Dip	Abdominals	Leg extension	Leg extension
Lat pullover	Leg press	Seated row	Hip extension	Hip extension
Chest press	Leg extension	Iso post delts	Hip flexion	Hip flexion
Chest cross	Leg curl	Lateral raise	Shin curl	Shin curl
Seated press	Hip adduction	Seated press	Toe raise	Toe raise
Lateral raise	Hip abduction	Lat pullover	Back extension	Back extension
Seated row	Shin curl	Lat pulldown	Abdominals	Abdominals
Shrug	Toe raise	Chest cross		
Dip	Back extension			
Abdominals	Abdominals			

*Including triceps and biceps will bring total sets to 20. Perform one set of each exercise for 14 to 18 total sets per routine.

Table 8.5 Upper and Lower Body Workouts for Aerobic–Anaerobic Sports

Upper body				
Routine 1	**Routine 2**	**Routine 3**	**Routine 4**	**Routine 5**
Chin-up	Chest press	Incline press	Seated press	Seated row
Lat pullover	Chest cross	Shrug	Lateral raise	Iso row
Chest cross	External rotator	Chest cross	External rotator	Lat pullover
Chest press	Lat pullover	Chest press	Iso row	Chin-up
Iso row	Chin-up	Seated row	Seated row	Chest press
Seated row	Shrug	Iso row	Shrug	Chest cross
Seated press	Lateral raise	Seated press	Chin-up	Shrug
Lateral raise	Seated press	Frontal raise	Lat pullover	Internal rotator
Shrug	Iso row	Lat pullover	Chest press	Seated press
Incline press	Seated row	Chin-up	Chest cross	Frontal raise
Biceps	Triceps	Triceps	Biceps	Biceps
Triceps	Biceps	Biceps	Triceps	Triceps
Abdominals	Abdominals	Abdominals	Abdominals	Abdominals
Lower body				
Routine 1	**Routine 2**	**Routine 3**	**Routine 4**	**Routine 5**
Leg press	Leg press	Leg press	Leg press	Leg press
Leg curl	Leg extension	Hip extension	Leg press	Hip extension
Leg extension	Hip extension	Leg press	Hip extension	Hip adduction
Hip extension	Hip flexion	Leg extension	Leg curl	Leg extension
Hip flexion	Leg curl	Hip flexion	Hip adduction	Leg curl
Hip adduction	Hip abduction	Lower back ext.	Leg extension	Hip flexion
Hip abduction	Leg press	Leg curl	Hip flexion	Hip abduction
Leg press	Lower back ext.	Hip adduction	Leg press	Lower back ext.
Toe raise	Hip adduction	Hip abduction	Hip abduction	Leg press
Shin curl	Toe raise	Shin curl	Toe raise	Shin curl
Lower back ext.	Shin curl	Toe raise	Shin curl	Toe raise

training that increases the ability to achieve explosive power and replenishes ATP and CP during brief recovery periods. Anaerobic athletes must be in superior anaerobic condition and prepared to neutralize high levels of lactic acid. Superior anaerobic condition requires training regularly with high-intensity intervals and HIT strength training. In most cases, athletes will have to perform multiple short, explosive, repeated all-out efforts at 100 percent of their max HR with intermittent breaks. These types of sports usually have a half time break ranging from 15 to 20 minutes.

The primary energy system for anaerobic athletes is glycolytic with moderate levels of lactic acid buffering. These athletes participate in sports that involve multiple high-intensity efforts. Their genetic profile is a combination of the mesomorph and endomorph body types, and most have a higher percentage of fast-twitch (type II) muscle fibers to enable high levels of power and speed.

Anaerobic athletes can benefit from using different strength training guidelines than athletes who participate in aerobic or mixed sports. The recommended rep range for athletes who participate in anaerobic endurance sports is 8 to 12 reps to MMF; however, this type of athlete can also benefit from rep ranges between 12 and 15 reps to push the muscle tissue into an extended MMF set and from rep ranges between 6 and 8 reps to help shock the neurological system.

Follow these strength training guidelines:

▶ Aim for a time under tension between 48 and 72 seconds.

▶ Increase the weight by 3 to 5 percent when 12 reps are reached or time under tension is greater than 72 seconds.

▶ Perform one to three sets per exercise.

▶ Allow 75 to 90 seconds of recovery between sets.

▶ Perform two to three upper body workouts per week, each totaling 12 to 16 sets of exercises, and two to three lower body workouts per week, each totaling 12 to16 sets of exercises, or perform two to three full body workouts per week, each totaling 20 to 24 sets of exercises.

▶ Use AOT on a regular basis, a maximum of one time weekly for each targeted muscle group, to facilitate maximum strength gains.

▶ Follow the strength routines shown in tables 8.6 and 8.7.

ANAEROBIC ATP-CP SPORTS

Anaerobic ATP-CP sports require athletes to exert 100 percent maximum effort, sometimes repeatedly, during an event or bout that lasts between 1 and 10 seconds and often has a recovery period greater than 10 minutes and sometimes even longer than 20 minutes. This extended recovery

Table 8.6 Routines for Anaerobic Sports*

1-Set routine (14 exercises, 14 sets)	2-Set routine (8 exercises, 14 sets)	3-Set routine (6 exercises, 14 sets)
Lat pulldown (M)	Lat pulldown (M)	Lat pulldown (M)
Lat pullover (S)	Lat pulldown (M)	Lat pulldown (M)
Chest press (M)	Chest press (M)	Lat pulldown (M)
Chest cross (S)	Chest press (M)	Chest press (M)
Seated row (M)	Seated row (M)	Chest press (M)
Iso seated row (S)	Seated row (M)	Chest press (M)
Seated press (M)	Seated press (M)	Seated row (M)
Lateral raise (S)	Seated press (M)	Seated row (M)
Incline row (M)	Low row (M)	Seated row (M)
Iso incline row (S)	Low row (M)	Seated press (M)
Incline press (M)	Incline press (M)	Seated press (M)
Incline cross (S)	Incline press (M)	Seated press (M)
Biceps curl (S)	Biceps curl (S)	Biceps curl (S)
Triceps extension (S)	Triceps extension (S)	Triceps extension (S)

(S) = Single-joint exercise; (M) = Multijoint exercise

*Perform one set of each exercise for 14 sets per total routine.

period allows plenty of time for the athlete to replenish ATP and CP stores. Sports that fall into this category include power lifting, weightlifting, shot-putting, discus throwing, high jumping, pole vaulting, and the 100-meter dash. Athletes who participate in these types of activities will tap primarily into the ATP-CP energy system and, therefore, must train to build maximum strength so that they can produce maximum explosive power. Anaerobic ATP-CP athletes use a primary energy system of short-term ATP-CP. The genetic profile of this type of athlete is primarily a combination of the mesomorph and endomorph body types or of the mesomorph and ectomorph body types, and these athletes have a high percentage of fast-twitch (type II) muscle fibers that produce explosive power.

Strength training guidelines for athletes who participate in anaerobic ATP-CP sports include recommended rep ranges of four to eight reps to MMF. Athletes or lifters who are unfamiliar with the effort associated with low-rep ranges could be prone to injury. Exceeding eight reps occasionally is recommended, but it is not recommended that athletes perform

Table 8.7 Lower Body Workouts for Anaerobic Sports*

Routine 1	Routine 2	Routine 3	Routine 4
Leg press A (M)	Leg press A (M)	Leg press B (M)	Leg extension (S)
Leg extension (S)	Leg press A (M)	Leg press A (M)	Leg extension (S)
Leg curl (S)	Leg curl (S)	Leg press A (M)	Leg press A (M)
Lunge (M)	Leg curl (S)	Hip extensor (S)	Leg curls (S)
Deadlift (M)	Leg extension (S)	Hip adductor (S)	Leg press A (M)
Hip extensor (S)	Leg extension (S)	Leg extension (S)	Leg curl (S)
Back extension (S)	Stiff-leg deadlift (S)	Leg extension (S)	Leg press A (M)
Hip abductor (S)	Deadlift (M)	Leg press B (M)	Hip extensor (S)
Hip adductor (S)	Hip adductor (S)	Back extension (S)	Hip extensor (S)
Hip flexor (S)	Hip extensor (S)	Back extension (S)	Hip flexor (S)
Ankle flexion (S)	Hip abductor (S)	Hip flexor (S)	Hip flexor (S)
Ankle extension (S)	Leg press B (M)	Hip abductor (S)	Deadlift (M)
	Ankle extension (S)	Deadlift (M)	Deadlift (M)
	Ankle flexion (S)	Deadlift (M)	Deadlift (M)
		Ankle flexion (S)	Back extension (S)
			Ankle extension (S)

(S) = Single-joint exercise; (M) = Multijoint exercise

*Perform one set of each exercise per routine.

fewer than four reps. These athletes may take full advantage of AOT once a week.

Follow these strength training guidelines:

- ▶ Aim for a time under tension between 24 and 48 seconds.
- ▶ Increase the weight by 3 to 5 percent when eight reps are reached or the time under tension is greater than 48 seconds.
- ▶ Perform one to three sets per exercise.
- ▶ Allow two to three minutes of recovery between sets.
- ▶ Perform two upper body workouts per week, each totaling 14 to 18 sets of exercises.
- ▶ Perform two lower body workouts per week, each totaling 14 to 18 sets of exercises.

▶ Perform two full body workouts per week, each totaling 22 to 26 sets of exercises.

▶ Use AOT on a regular basis.

▶ Follow the strength routines shown in tables 8.6 and 8.7.

The recommended strength training protocols found in this chapter are not etched in stone and can be adjusted to meet the demands of different sports, as in the example with the golfer and the shot-putter at the beginning of this chapter, who may tap into the same energy systems but who require dramatically different functional power and strength. In addition, the energy requirements within the same sport can differ greatly depending on positions. For example, a soccer goalie taps primarily into the anaerobic energy system, while the sweeper uses both the aerobic and anaerobic systems. Although both players participate in the same sport, their overall training programs would differ slightly because they perform different activities on the field.

After reviewing this chapter, you should have an expanded understanding of how the body's energy systems function and how they relate to sport-specific lifting protocols. In general, the more directly you target the energy needs and enhanced energy storage training response associated with your sport, the greater the potential for excelling in that sport.

Advanced Overload Training

Now that you've learned how to implement the HIT principles and design a program, you can learn how to take athletic performance to the next level by applying advanced overload training (AOT). An important component of the HIT strength system is pushing the body to 100 percent momentary muscular failure (MMF) on every set, which many athletes are able to achieve without AOT. Other athletes, however, have the desire and sport-specific strength needs to push beyond MMF to reach deeper into the muscle tissue for increased protein degradation. The safest and most effective way to do this is through AOT. Although genetic predisposition determines the level of maximum strength and muscle hypertrophy, or bulk, that each athlete is able to achieve, each athlete dedicated to the HIT system will experience measurable increases in strength. These strength gains are even more apparent when AOT is incorporated into the program. It is critical that AOT be carefully administered under the direct supervision of a HIT specialist to ensure safe one-on-one spotting techniques. The success of AOT is largely based on the training partner's ability to perform perfect spots and to motivate the athlete to push beyond the present pain threshold.

Finding a HIT Specialist

Learning from a specialist who understands advanced overload training is important for safety. To find a specialist in your area who is familiar with the HIT system, programming, and AOT, contact the NSPA headquarters at 800-494-6772 or go to www.nspainc.com.

Numerous advanced overload training techniques are available, but the following eight are the safest and most effective: assisted positive repetitions, forced negative resistance, breakdowns, multiple-set combinations, slow training, quarter and half reps, MMF isometric pauses, and manual resistance (see chapter 11 for instruction on performing manuals).

After using the HIT system for an entire year, athletes can assess the year's athletic performance and strength achievements and make appropriate adjustments for the upcoming off-season periodization plan. Most athletes prefer to reach a maximum strength plateau with MMF before adding AOT to the program. When AOT is added, it should be used only once a week because of the three- to four-day recovery time needed. Once the desired level of strength is achieved with AOT, the goal is to maintain it throughout the entire season. The bottom line during the season is to maintain lifting intensity to avoid strength loss, as discussed in chapter 5.

Some dedicated athletes may feel compelled to use AOT during every workout and may train with it three times a week. Their intentions are to speed up the strength-building process and achieve a competitive edge; however, such ambitious training with AOT can have the opposite effect over time and can lead to overtraining symptoms. To be successful with AOT, athletes must remember that recovery is just as important as the overload itself; there is a point where an overdose of overload and inadequate recovery affect progress negatively. This overdose can happen during a workout and or over a period of weeks. Remember, it's better to be overrested than overtrained.

ASSISTED POSITIVE REPETITIONS

Assisted positive repetitions are commonly used with AOT, but they require a skilled HIT spotter with experience. The lifter will determine a rep range and perform perfect reps to MMF. As the lifter approaches positive failure during the last rep, the spotter must be prepared to manually assist with the weight by keeping it moving at a slow, controlled rate; too much assistance will inhibit the recruitment of fibers and too little assistance will stop the weight. This is why it is critical to have a skilled spotter who understands the relationship between time under tension and speed of movement for maximum activation of all fibers throughout the full range of motion. It is also important for both the spotter and the lifter to know that the negative aspect is approximately 40 percent stronger than the positive because of increased internal muscle friction. Even though the negative is performed more slowly than the positive (typically three to four seconds for the negative and two to three seconds for the positive), it will not reach failure first.

Upon completing the assisted positive rep, the lifter performs a slow, controlled, six- to eight-second negative. Because failure has not yet been

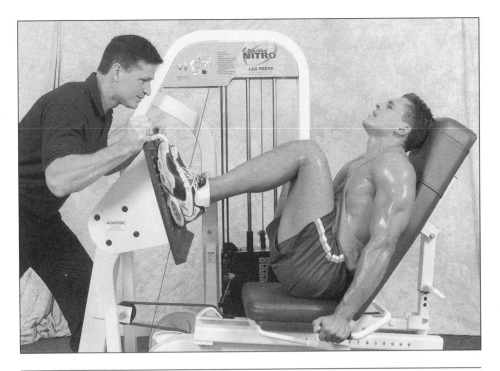

AOT will help break through strength plateaus and reach maximum genetic strength potential.

reached during the negative phase, the goal is to perform three to four additional slow negative reps to accomplish negative failure with the same weight. The lifter will get progressively weaker during the positive phase of the reps that precede the negative, which means that the spotter will need to lift more of the weight with each consecutive rep. It's beneficial for the lift to continue, despite the weakened positive phase, because the athlete still has the ability to exert effort during the negative phase of the remaining reps. Only unassisted positive repetitions are recorded on the training chart.

Caution: To protect the lower back from strain, the spotter should be in a stable position when assisting with the additional reps. The spotter should also be prepared to lift the entire weight when the athlete reaches complete MMF on the positive. Machines are often a safer modality for this type of AOT.

FORCED NEGATIVE RESISTANCE

The goal of forced negative resistance AOT is to achieve both positive and negative muscle failure simultaneously. For example, a lifter may use a weight that will bring positive failure in 10 reps. The spotter applies additional negative resistance during the last four or five reps. This additional resistance begins after the full positive contraction; it starts during the distinct isometric pause and is continued throughout the full range of the negative phase of the rep. The additional negative resistance should be smooth and consistent with the natural strength curve or cam. This application takes practice and is much more effective when training partners are familiar with each other's strength levels and tolerance. If the additional negative resistance is appropriate, the lifter will ideally reach failure during both the positive and negative phases within the desired rep range. It is hard to measure the exact amount of forced negative resistance to be applied, but, if quantified, it would likely be between 30 and 40 percent of the positive resistance being used. The additional negative resistance activates greater fiber recruitment, which causes the negative and positive failure to occur simultaneously. Keep in mind that the spotter must know exactly how to perform this AOT to achieve maximum results safely.

BREAKDOWN TRAINING: THE STRIP-SET TECHNIQUE

Breakdown training enables an athlete to exceed the point of positive MMF and extend the set to recruit additional muscle fibers. The goal of this challenging AOT technique is to activate every muscle fiber, including both fast- and slow-twitch. The breakdown technique is applied at the end of a set when the muscles have reached positive failure. At this point, the athlete or spotter reduces the resistance by 25 to 30 percent, taking no longer than five seconds to reduce the weight. The set is then continued with perfect reps for another two to four reps until failure occurs again. This should be repeated for two to three additional short sets, depending on the level of tissue breakdown desired (see table 9.1). The amount of weight reduction can vary, depending on the athlete's muscle endurance and pain threshold. The advantage of this technique is that the athlete can perform breakdowns even when training alone and with all types of strength modalities.

Table 9.1   Breakdown Training Technique

Length of rest interval	Approximate reduction in weight
0-10 sec.	25-30%
10-20 sec.	20-25%
20-30 sec.	15-20%
30-40 sec.	10-15%

MULTIPLE-SET COMBINATIONS

As discussed in chapter 7, multiple sets can be used in many different ways as a form of AOT. It's best to create six to eight routines that involve a variety of sets including single, double, and triple sets for the multijoint movements (see chapter 4). The following are multiple-set protocols that involve different recovery times, pre- and postexhaustion combinations, angle combinations, and exercise combinations.

10-8-6 or 6-6-6 Format

Any sequence of repetitions can be used with this format. The objective is to reach muscular failure at the repetitions specified for each set with a specific amount of recovery, generally between 30 and 60 seconds. For example, for 10-8-6, the goal of the first set is to achieve failure at 10 reps. The athlete recovers for 30 to 60 seconds and then reduces the weight to achieve eight reps on the next set, recovers 30 to 60 seconds and again reduces the weight to achieve six reps on the third set. The athlete determines the specific weight reduction. Keep in mind that all athletes respond differently to this type of overload stimulus, so the weight reduction will vary accordingly. Table 9.2 presents a sample 10-8-6 sequence.

Table 9.2 10-8-6 Rep Sequence Training

Set no.	Repetitions	Approximate weight reduction	Rest intervals
1	10	10-15%	30-60 sec.
2	8	5-10%	30-60 sec.
3	6		

Single-Multi-Single Format

This multiple-set, pre- and postexhaustion combination uses alternating single-multi-single-joint combinations. The athlete performs a single-joint, preexhaustion exercise, follows it with a multijoint exercise that works the same muscle group, and then finishes with a single-joint, postexhaustion exercise. For example, the order could be lateral raise, seated press, and lateral raise. The timing of rest intervals between sets is determined by the athlete's goals. Recovery time adds another significant variable to this sequence of multiple sets and must be taken into consideration when deciding what weights to use.

Multi-Single-Multi Format

This multiple-set, post- and preexhaustion combination uses a multi-single-multi-joint combination. The athlete starts with a multijoint exercise, follows with a single-joint exercise working the same muscle group, and then finishes with a multijoint exercise working the same muscle group. One combination is lat pulldown, lat pullover, and lat pulldown. Rest intervals are determined according to the athlete's goals. Again, recovery time adds another significant variable.

Multi-Set Angles

Multiple sets with different angles work the same muscle group with 15- to 20-degree angle changes (see table 9.3). For instance, an athlete may perform three sets of the single-joint chest cross, with the cables at a different angle for each set. Again, recovery time can vary according to the athlete's goals.

Table 9.3 Multiple Set Angles

Smith machine/multi-angled bench
Bench 110°
Bench 90°
Bench 70°
Cable chest cross/Free Motion cable
Chest cross 110°
Chest cross 90°
Chest cross 70°

SLOW TRAINING

Slow training (ST) can be effective with all athletes, especially those who are rehabilitating from an injury or who do not want to place heavy loads on the joints. ST has also been shown to be very effective with athletes who are training for endurance sports that require a great deal of muscle endurance and stamina. This is because ST allows athletes to use less weight—and therefore produce less joint trauma—and still achieve MMF within the desired time under tension. Ken Hutchins' super-slow training technique recommends that the positive phase be 10 seconds and the negative phase 4 seconds. NSPA has used several ST protocols with a wide variety of athletes and found that, although most athletes like the variety, they do not have the patience to train with 14-second reps on a consistent basis.

Each rep must be performed in deliberately exaggerated slow motion while executing perfect form. This requires a great deal of discipline and concentration, and a partner or trainer who can provide motivation and keep the lifter from breaking form. The ST protocol also requires a training partner with a watch who will keep the athlete within the recommended rep times. One advantage of ST is that it minimizes momentum to facilitate maximum muscle fiber recruitment. One set of four to eight reps should be performed to failure within 60 to 120 seconds. Table 9.4 illustrates several slow-training protocols that can be used to add variety to the AOT slow rep.

Table 9.4 HIT Slow-Training Technique

Positive phase (lifting)	Negative phase (lowering)
6-8 sec.	6-8 sec.
10 sec. (Hutchins' super-slow protocol)	4 sec.
3-4 sec.	8-10 sec.

QUARTER AND HALF REPETITIONS

Quarter and half repetitions are performed toward the end of a set, during the positive or negative phase of an exercise, to increase overload and muscle recruitment in that specific degree of lifting angle. For example, in the biceps curl, an athlete might perform 10 reps to MMF and, on the negative phase of the eighth rep, stop one-quarter of the way down, make a concentric contraction, and then return to the fully contracted position. At this point, the lifter pauses for one second and then lowers the weight to full extension. The quarter repetition at the top of the lift can be repeated several times, if desired. Half repetitions are performed in the same manner, except that the repeating increment equals half the distance of the rep. The integration of quarter reps and half reps does not replace or compromise the concept of full range of motion strength training; it is simply another HIT technique to shock the targeted muscle or muscles during a specific movement.

MMF ISOMETRIC PAUSES

MMF isometric pauses occur during the last rep. The skills of the spotter are most challenged with this AOT technique. When the lifter reaches MMF on the positive aspect of the last rep, the spotter instructs the lifter to apply an isometric pause for one to two seconds. Then the spotter assists with the positive. This process continues through two or three distinct pauses, or sticking points. The same protocol can be applied to the negative aspect of the lift, with emphasis on forced negative resistance while performing three to four isometric pauses.

MANUAL RESISTANCE

Manual resistance is a favorite AOT technique, but learning how to apply manual resistance, or manuals, is difficult to master—it takes numerous hours of practice to perfect. Manuals must be taught by a HIT specialist who is well versed with the correct technique and application. Many athletes learn manuals incorrectly and then perfect bad habits. If manuals are not applied correctly, the athlete will not receive the full benefit and injury may result.

Manuals are performed without strength training equipment. The spotter applies the resistance necessary to achieve complete 100 percent MMF for both the positive and negative phases of the rep. For manuals

Manual strength training is the single greatest tool that athletes possess.

to be effective, the athlete and spotter must work together as a team and communicate during the set while trying to achieve failure within the designated rep range.

For example, the athlete may perform single-joint isolated lateral raises, working the medial deltoids, while sitting down with back support and maintaining good posture, with both arms bent at 90 degrees. The spotter—a HIT specialist—stands behind the athlete and applies direct variable resistance to both elbows through the full range of motion. The spotter is aware that a unique angular strength curve is involved and the resistance must be applied equally on both elbows as the athlete begins to raise the arms to a horizontal position. The athlete raises the arms through the positive phase of the lift with 100 percent effort while the spotter pushes down on the elbows with resistance that controls the speed of movement to three to four seconds until full range of motion is achieved. When the elbows reach the horizontal position, the spotter continues to apply resistance as the athlete pauses in an isometric contraction for a half count. At this point, the spotter must apply 30 to 40 percent more resistance during the negative phase of the rep.

The athlete must resist with 100 percent effort during the negative phase. The spotter is responsible for controlling the speed of the negative, which should be between three and four seconds. The goal is to exhaust the medial deltoids through the positive and negative phases between 10 and 15 reps, or 60 to 90 seconds of time under tension.

If done correctly, manual resistance provides the most intense overload training athletes can experience. However, there are some limitations. One of the drawbacks to manual training is the strength needed by the spotter to effectively apply the required resistance. The athlete may have to start out with 80 percent effort during the first three to four reps and gradually work toward 100 percent effort. If there are significant strength differences between the spotter and the lifter, the spotter will have to be creative with manipulating body weight, using iso-lateral movements, using the full arm for leverage as opposed to the elbow, and using tools such as ropes or towels to assist with the movement.

One of the enjoyments HIT specialists experience is teaching AOT to motivated athletes. Instantly they become psyched to experiment and implement the new AOT applications. They must keep in mind, though, that these techniques require a HIT specialist and longer recovery periods. The AOT applications are designed to take athletes to the next level of strength gains and help push them through strength plateaus. AOT should be used with all lifts during a workout to avoid the risk of overlapping muscle groups with inadequate recovery periods. The ultimate success of the HIT program and AOT is based on athletes' motivation to learn the system and techniques. It also depends on the athletes' ability to adjust the program as their bodies adapt and mature with the specialized training.

10

Precision Exercise Technique

IT-educated athletes excel in numerous ways. They can easily analyze strength movements and devices and are able to immediately recognize incorrect techniques and faulty biomechanics. They also have a competitive edge, which enables them to maximize their athletic strength potential by becoming independent thinkers. Because of their specialized training, they are comfortable challenging and intelligently discussing strength training theories and applications with their peers and coaches. And they can use their knowledge of muscle physiology, exercise science, and proper biomechanics to develop training programs to meet performance goals and properly rehabilitate if injured. In fact, these athletes often become ambassadors of the HIT system and are motivated to help others also develop safe and effective training regimes.

Most athletes are introduced to numerous strength programs and lifting techniques throughout their careers and have to make a decision about which path to follow. The information contained in this book will help athletes determine the safest and most productive approach for training and will establish the foundation for staying healthy beyond their years in competitive sports.

This chapter will provide an overview of spotting, stretching, muscle movement analysis, and correct biomechanical movements. Figures 10.1 and 10.2 show muscles in the body that will be used in the exercises in chapters 10 and 11. Refer to these diagrams for any questions about muscle usage in different exercises.

The success of the HIT strength system relies on the athlete's ability to work extremely hard during every set and workout, as well as the spotter's ability to provide effective guidance during the lift and with AOT. This success can be further enhanced when the HIT athlete incorporates into the

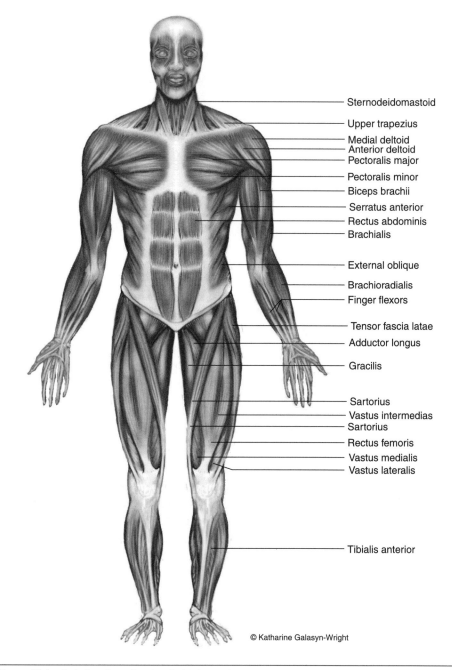

Sternodeidomastoid

Upper trapezius

Medial deltoid
Anterior deltoid
Pectoralis major

Pectoralis minor

Biceps brachii

Serratus anterior

Rectus abdominis

Brachialis

External oblique

Brachioradialis

Finger flexors

Tensor fascia latae

Adductor longus

Gracilis

Sartorius

Vastus intermedias

Sartorius

Rectus femoris

Vastus medialis

Vastus lateralis

Tibialis anterior

© Katharine Galasyn-Wright

Figure 10.1 Anterior view of major skeletal muscles.

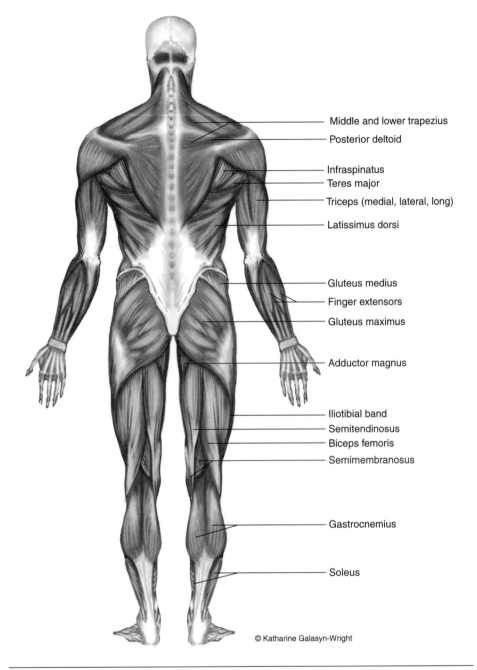

Middle and lower trapezius
Posterior deltoid

Infraspinatus
Teres major
Triceps (medial, lateral, long)
Latissimus dorsi

Gluteus medius
Finger extensors
Gluteus maximus

Adductor magnus

Iliotibial band
Semitendinosus
Biceps femoris
Semimembranosus

Gastrocnemius

Soleus

© Katharine Galasyn-Wright

Figure 10.2 Posterior view of major skeletal muscles.

"training formula" such components as a balanced diet, proper hydration with electrolytes, adequate sleep, flexibility, and supplements.

THE ART OF SPOTTING

The HIT system requires precise spotting skills and attention to detail during each rep and every set to achieve maximum strength results. The perfect spot is actually an extended ergogenic aid under the HIT system. The art of spotting is not an easy skill to learn and requires many hours of practice under the instruction of a HIT specialist. Many athletes don't recognize the difference between a poorly spotted lift and one that is smoothly guided through a full range of motion. As a result, poor spotting skills are overlooked, and the athlete's workout becomes less than optimal because of improper spotting techniques. With the perfect spot, the athlete feels as though the spotter never touches the weight and continues through the range of motion with smooth guidance. The spotter facilitates muscle recruitment by assisting only enough to keep the weight from stopping and never takes control of the weight during the rep unless there is absolute need at MMF. Experience shows that once athletes experience the perfect spot, they will accept nothing less and would rather have no spot than a bad one.

Most athletes have had negative experiences in partner spotting techniques. First, there is the preoccupied spotter, who is worried about personal concerns and lacks the motivation to spot the training partner. If a spot is offered, it is far from adequate, and the spotter would have been of more use attending to those personal issues. Then there is the "sorry" spotter. This person tries to assist when it is too late and then succeeds in taking the resistance away completely. In other words, the spotter overassists by helping too much, which inevitably shuts down the tension to the working muscles. The commonly heard response for this type of spotter is "sorry." Or an athlete might have a clueless spotter, who has no idea which is the positive and which is the negative phase, thus adding or taking away tension at the wrong time and in the wrong direction. A dangerous spotter is one who reads about and tries to assist with AOT without any experience or understanding of the applications, and will most likely hurt those he is spotting. Another bad spot typically happens when three or more athletes are training together and assumptions lead to inadequate or lack of spotting. For example, the lifter reaches MMF while each spotter assumes the other one is the one assisting with the lift. Suddenly they all exclaim, "I thought you had it!" Unfortunately, this assumption can get an athlete injured quickly.

The art of spotting is not a skill that comes easily; it takes many hours of instruction from a skilled spotter and regular practice to master the skills. Once mastered, however, the spotter's skills can easily enhance an athlete's strength training program by contributing as much as a 5 percent increase in overall strength gains.

What constitutes a perfect spot? First, the spotter must ensure that the lifter is 100 percent safe at all times while performing perfect reps. When the lifter approaches the end of a set, it is critical that the spotter encourage perfect form and guide the lifter through the last two to four reps without causing a break in perfect form. When the lifter has reached MMF, a spotter who is skilled in the spotting technique associated with AOT may choose to transition the lift into a full AOT. The goal is always to safely raise the bar to the next level. Athletes who choose to perform AOT must have complete confidence in their partners' spotting ability, or injuries may result. The perfect spot includes the following:

- ▶ The spotter must make sure that the appropriate weight is being used, check for collars on the bar, and clear the lifting area of obstructions in case the weight is released.
- ▶ The spotter must be positioned to safely rack the weight or guide the weight away from the lifter if necessary.
- ▶ The spotter must avoid touching the bar or weight if not needed.
- ▶ The spotter's body must not be positioned in a way that makes the lifter feel uncomfortable or overcrowded.
- ▶ The spotter must provide only enough assistance to keep the resistance moving. Too much assistance will take away potential fiber recruitment, and not enough assistance will impede fluid movement of the rep.
- ▶ The spotter must understand the biomechanics of the lift and make sure that perfect form is not compromised during any part of the set.
- ▶ The spotter must understand when and how to apply AOT.

HIT strength athletes learn how to tap into the adrenaline surge when they experience muscle fatigue, putting mind over matter, and they count on a perfect spot to motivate them to go beyond perceived failure. The goal of the spotter working with a HIT strength athlete is not only to guide the lift but to also push the lifter beyond the point where no assistance is required. Together, the lifter and spotter can raise the bar for a set and go an additional two to three reps, even when the lifter's mind is saying, *No more!* This type of training undoubtedly creates the competitive edge and reinforces the need for a skilled spotter to facilitate the lift and motivate the athlete.

PROPER FLEXIBILITY, WARM-UP, AND COOL-DOWN

Dr. Wayne Westcott's research has demonstrated that strength training followed by a flexibility program causes greater muscle growth than just strength training alone. Following are recommendations for safe and effective stretching.

▸ Never stretch a cold muscle.

▸ Always perform 5 to 10 minutes of easy cardiovascular exercise, such as walking on a treadmill, before stretching.

▸ Perform a static 30- to 40-second stretch two to three times for each muscle group daily.

▸ Incorporate proprioceptive neuromuscular facilitation (PNF) stretching, which takes two people and a clear understanding of the neurophysiology mechanisms involved with the techniques. (Sample protocol: passive contraction for three seconds, hold for three seconds, slow release for three seconds, relax for four seconds, then repeat up to three times.) Experience has shown PNF stretching to be the most effective way to increase an athletes' flexibility. Ideally a HIT specialist with PNF training will supervise and administer the PNF stretch.

▸ Perform static stretches after a cardiovascular warm-up for 15 to 20 minutes before practice and 10 to 15 minutes after practice.

MUSCLE MOVEMENT ANALYSIS

There are several types of muscle resistance for training, including isometric, isotonic, and isokinetic. Each of these can be performed with different machines or alternate methods, which creates many choices for the HIT athlete.

Isometric contraction occurs when the contracting forces are equal to the resistance or are being maximally applied to a fixed immovable object, or both. There is no joint movement, and the muscle length remains unchanged. The isometric contraction can be used at different angles during the concentric or eccentric phase of a rep to elicit greater tension. It is recommended as an AOT technique during the last few reps before MMF.

Isotonic resistance remains constant throughout the movement; however, the muscle force output varies according to its mechanical leverage. The inherent limitation of a muscle's mechanical leverage—its sticking point—is most apparent when performing isotonic exercises, such as lifting free weights. "Cable" isotonic machine resistance varies according to the number of pulleys and the positioning of the pulleys associated with the movement, but it does not vary the resistance according to a natural strength curl. "Cam" isotonic machine resistance is preset by the cam device on the machine. The cam then varies the resistance throughout the full range of motion according to a generic strength curve predetermined by the manufacturer, such as Nautilus or Strive. "Lever" isotonic machine resistance is preset by the machine's lever arms. The levers then vary the resistance throughout the full range of motion according to a generic strength curve predetermined by the manufacturer, such as Hammer or Power Plus.

Resistance from a cam or cable pivoting isotonic machine varies according to the predetermined cam and the angle of the pulley cable, based on its pivoting axle. The cam and pivoting pulley vary resistance throughout the full range of motion according to the angles of pull, such as with Ground Zero's Free Motion equipment. Concentric isokinetic machines apply resistance only through the concentric contraction, and the speed of movement is set by the athlete. The speed is constant through the full range of motion, and the force output is determined by the athlete's ability to apply maximum force against the pad through the full range of motion, as with Kieser or Kin Com equipment. Concentric/eccentric isokinetic machine resistance is both concentric and eccentric, and the speed is predetermined. The force output, however, is dictated by the athlete. Examples include equipment from Kieser or Kin Com. Manual isokinetic resistance is applied by a training partner during both the concentric and eccentric phases. The partner dictates the amount of resistance, and the athlete performs 100 percent effort throughout the full range of motion.

CORRECT BIOMECHANICAL MOVEMENTS

It is common to see athletes perform strength movements, learned from others, that apply unnecessary and repetitive stress to the joints, which may eventually lead to injury. Therefore, athletes must be able to distinguish between a sound strength movement and those movements that negatively overload the joint and lead to overuse injuries. Follow the exercise descriptions carefully to avoid injury.

UPPER BODY PUSH MOVEMENTS: MULTIJOINT AND SINGLE-JOINT

Dumbbell Bench Press

Primary Movers: pectoralis major, anterior deltoid, triceps

Type of Movement: compound, multijoint, linear

Technique

Lying down on the bench with feet flat on the floor, grip the dumbbells approximately shoulder-width apart and push the weight directly over the chest until the elbows are just shy of locking. Pause. Lower the weight to the starting position and again pause. Always maintain a neutral arch in the lower back and a neutral wrist, and keep the forearms perpendicular to the floor. Repeat. When using dumbbells, seek the assistance of a spotter; otherwise injury may occur.

a

b

Dumbbell Chest Fly

Primary Movers: pectoralis major, anterior deltoid

Type of Movement: single joint, isolation, rotary

Technique

Lying back on the bench, extend the arms to the side with elbows bent at approximately 45 degrees, and hold the dumbbells perpendicular to the floor. Bring the arms together vertically in front of the chest until the dumbbells touch and pause. Slowly lower the dumbbells to the starting position. Always keep the shoulder, elbow, and wrist joint directly in line. If there is abnormal joint stress, avoid this exercise. Repeat.

a

b

Cable Chest Cross

Primary Movers: pectoralis major, anterior deltoid

Type of Movement: single joint, isolation, rotary

Technique

Stand in a straddle position with feet approximately shoulder-width apart, and lean the upper torso slightly forward over the hips with arms stretched out horizontally and elbows slightly bent. Grab the cable handles with a full grip and palms perpendicular to the floor. Bring the arms together in front of the chest until the hands touch and pause. Then slowly control the cables as they return to the starting position and pause. Repeat.

a

b

Dumbbell Decline Press

Primary Movers: pectoralis major, anterior deltoid, triceps

Type of Movement: compound, multijoint, linear

Technique

Lying back on the bench with feet flat on the floor if possible, grip the dumbbells approximately shoulder-width apart and push the weight directly over the chest straight to the ceiling until the elbows are just shy of locking, then pause. Lower the weight to the starting position and pause. Always maintain a neutral arch in the lower back and a neutral wrist, and keep the forearms perpendicular to the floor. Repeat.

Because this position may cause increased blood flow to the head, sensations of dizziness and lightheadedness may result, so be careful when standing up after the exercise. And seek the assistance of a spotter when using dumbbells, or injury may occur.

a

b

Cable Decline Chest Cross

Primary Movers: pectoralis major, anterior deltoid

Type of Movement: single joint, isolation, rotary

Technique

Stand with feet approximately shoulder-width apart and lean the upper torso slightly forward over the hips with arms stretched out horizontally and the elbows slightly bent. Grab the cable handles with a full grip and palms horizontal to floor, and bring the arms together in a down position in front of the pelvis until the hands touch, then pause. Then slowly control the cables as they return to the starting position and pause. Repeat.

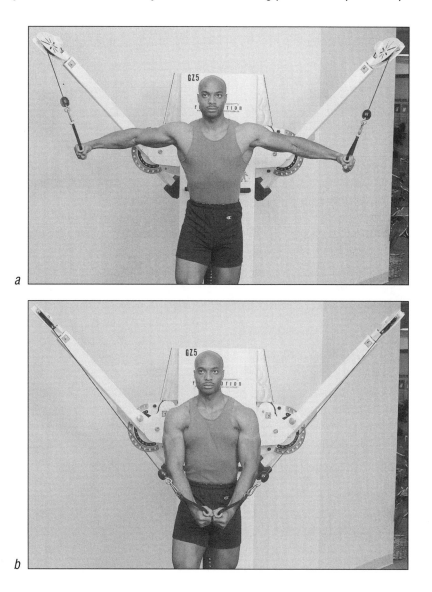

a

b

Dumbbell Incline Press

Primary Movers: anterior deltoid, pectoralis major, triceps

Type of Movement: compound, multijoint, linear

Technique

Lying back on the incline bench at a 135-degree incline, feet flat on the floor, grip the dumbbells approximately shoulder-width apart and push the weight directly over the chest straight to the ceiling until the elbows are just shy of locking, then pause. Lower the weight to the starting position and pause. Always maintain a neutral arch in the lower back and a neutral wrist, and keep the forearms perpendicular to the floor. Repeat. Seek the assistance of a spotter when using dumbbells; otherwise injury may occur.

a

b

Cable Frontal Raise

Primary Movers: anterior deltoid, pectoralis major

Type of Movement: single joint, isolation, rotary

Technique

Stand on a stable position with the feet shoulder width apart and grasp the cable handles with a full pronated grip, approximately 20 degrees behind the torso. Raise the handles in front of the body, just above the chest and parallel to the floor, then pause. Lower the handles to the starting position and pause. Repeat. For variety, hands can be in a pronated or parallel position. Always maintain a neutral arch in the lower back and a neutral wrist.

a

b

Dumbbell Frontal Raise

Primary Movers: anterior deltoid, pectoralis major

Type of Movement: single joint, isolation, rotary

Technique

Lying back on the incline bench at a 135-degree incline, feet flat on the floor, hold the dumbbells with a full grip and place them at the same angle as the bench. Raise the dumbbells until the arms are perpendicular to the incline bench and pause. Lower the weight until it reaches the starting position and pause. Repeat. Hands may be in a pronated or parallel position. Always maintain a neutral arch in the lower back and a neutral wrist. Seek the assistance of a spotter when using dumbbells; otherwise injury may occur.

a

b

Cable Incline Chest Cross

Primary Movers: anterior deltoid, pectoralis major

Type of Movement: single joint, isolation, rotary

Technique

Stand in a straddle position with feet approximately shoulder-width apart and lean the upper torso slightly forward over the hips with the arms stretched out horizontally and elbows slightly bent. Grab the cable handles with a full grip and palms perpendicular to the floor. Bring the arms together overhead at a 45-degree angle in front of the chest until the hands touch, then pause. Then slowly control the cables as they return to the starting position and pause. Repeat.

a

b

Dumbbell Seated Press

Primary Movers: medial deltoids, anterior deltoid, triceps

Type of Movement: compound, multijoint, linear

Technique

Place the bench at a 10-degree angle, and sit with the back and head against the bench and feet flat on the floor. Grip the dumbbells approximately shoulder-width apart and push the weight directly overhead toward the ceiling until the elbows are just shy of locking, and pause. Lower the weight until it reaches the starting position and pause. Always maintain a neutral arch in the lower back and a neutral, rigid wrist, and keep the forearms perpendicular to the floor. Repeat. Seek the assistance of a spotter when using dumbbells, or injury may result. Variations for this exercise include placing the elbows in front of the chest to provide more anterior deltoid action or starting with internal rotation of the palms and ending with external rotation (often referred to as the "Arnold press").

a

b

Machine Lateral Raise

Primary Movers: medial deltoids

Type of Movement: single joint, isolation, rotary

Technique

Sit on a lateral raise machine with the back straight and feet flat on the floor. Raise the elbows to the side, shoulder level with elbows bent at 45 degrees. The forearms are parallel to the floor at the midpoint of the lift and held for a distinct pause. Lower the weight to the starting position with the elbows at the side of the body. Repeat. Push through the elbows at all times and avoid elevating the trapezius muscles during the movement. Maintain neutral wrists—never let them rotate up externally or rise above the elbow while performing the movement.

a

b

Seated Dip Hammer Press

Primary Movers: pectoralis major, anterior deltoid, triceps

Type of Movement: compound, multijoint, linear

Technique

Sit on the dip machine with feet flat on the floor, the back pressed against the pad, and the head and neck in a neutral position. At the start of the movement, the upper arms are parallel to the ground and the forearms are bent at approximately 45 degrees with the palms facing each other. Push down toward the floor until the elbows are just shy of locking, and pause. Then lower the weight until the forearms are at 45 degrees, then pause. Repeat. The hand position can be altered to a prone position if the shoulder girdle feels uncomfortable. Always keep a neutral arch in the lower back and a neutral wrist, and use a seat belt if available.

a

b

Body Weight Dip

Primary Movers: pectoralis major, anterior deltoid, triceps

Type of Movement: compound, multijoint, linear

Technique

Start with the arms bent at approximately 45 degrees and the palms facing each other. Press up toward the ceiling until the elbows are just shy of locking and pause. Then lower until the elbows are at 90 degrees and pause. Repeat. The hand position can be altered to a prone position if the shoulder girdle feels uncomfortable. Always maintain a neutral arch in the lower back and a neutral wrist, and never exceed the parallel upper arm position as this can lead to excessive shoulder stress.

a

b

Cable Triceps Extension

Primary Movers: long, medial, and lateral triceps extensors

Type of Movement: single joint, isolation, rotary

Technique

Stand straight up with a soft bend in the knees and flex at the elbows while grasping the handles diagonal to the floor. Push down toward the floor until the elbows are just shy of locking and pause. Slowly return to the starting position and pause. Repeat. Keep the neck and lower back in a neutral position. Additional grips can be used for this exercise but be sure to not compromise the full range of motion when using these grips.

a

b

Cable Kick-Back Triceps Extension

Primary Movers: long, medial, and lateral triceps extensors

Type of Movement: single joint, isolation, rotary

Technique

Standing in front of the cable, bend over with a flat back and a slight bend in the knees. Grab the cable with a prone grip with the elbow slightly higher than the back and fully flexed. Press the handle back until the elbow reaches full extension. While pressing back, make sure the body stays rigid and the elbow does not drift down toward the floor. Repeat. This exercise can also be performed with the palms perpendicular to the floor or supine to emphasize different triceps heads, but be sure not to compromise the full range of motion when using these grips.

a

b

UPPER BODY PULL MOVEMENTS: MULTIJOINT AND SINGLE-JOINT

Cable Seated Horizontal Row With Lat Emphasis

Primary Movers: latissimus dorsi, posterior deltoids, rhomboids, middle trapezius, biceps

Type of Movement: compound, multijoint, linear

Technique

Sitting with a slight bend in the hips and knees and feet pressed firmly onto the platform, grasp the handles with the palms perpendicular to the floor. Pull the handles toward the body in a straight line, with the elbows moving along the side of the body. Keep the forearms parallel to the floor and the wrists neutral. Squeeze at the full contraction with a pause. Then slowly return the handles to the starting position while gently straightening the elbows and keeping tension on the targeted muscles. Repeat. Keep the lower back rigid at all times and do not let the wrists flex, especially at the full contraction position. Adduct the scapula to increase shoulder activation.

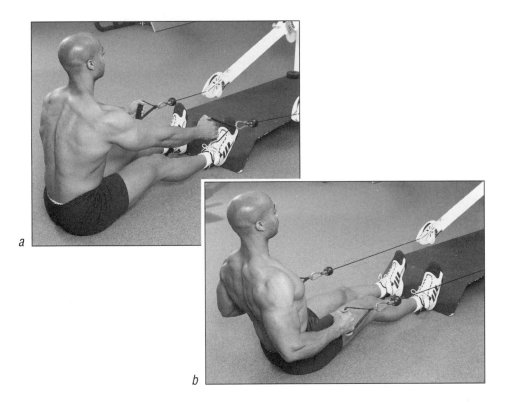

a

b

Cable Seated Row With Posterior Deltoid Emphasis

Primary Movers: latissimus dorsi, posterior deltoids, rhomboids, middle trapezius, biceps

Type of Movement: compound, multijoint, linear

Technique

Sitting with a slight bend in the hips and knees and feet pressed firmly onto the platform, grasp the handles with the arms and palms parallel to the floor. Pull the handles toward the body in a horizontal plane, and keep the wrists neutral. Squeeze at the full contraction with a pause. Then slowly return the handles to the starting position while gently straightening the elbows and keeping tension on the targeted muscles. Repeat. Keep the lower back rigid at all times and do not let the wrists flex, especially at the full contraction position. Adduct the scapula to increase shoulder activation.

a

b

Horizontal Pull-ups

Primary Movers: posterior deltoids, latissimus dorsi, biceps

Type of Movement: compound, multijoint, linear

Technique

Lie in a supine position with the feet on a stability ball and arms stretched out grasping the bar. Pull the body up to the bar, then pause at full contraction. Slowly lower the body down to the starting position while keeping constant tension on the targeted muscle groups.

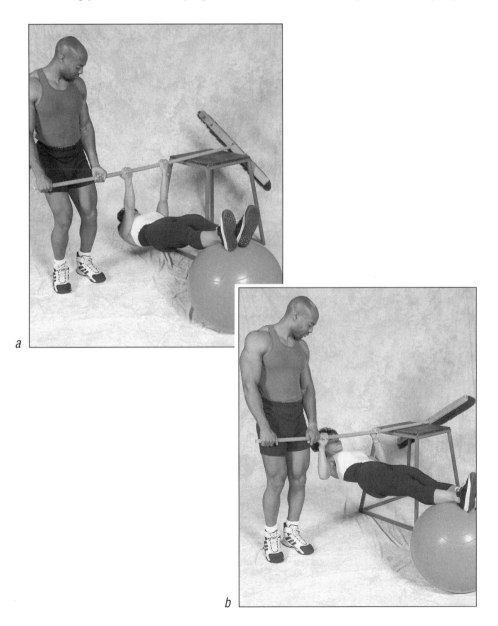

a

b

Prone Iso Post Delt

Primary Movers: latissimus dorsi, posterior deltoids

Type of Movement: single joint, isolation, rotary

Technique

Lie facedown on the machine with elbows bent at 90 degrees and pushing against the pads. Push the elbows up until they reach the full range of motion and pause. Lower the elbows slowly to the starting position while keeping tension on the targeted muscles at all times. Repeat. Each rep should reach the same spot at full range of motion, and the elbow should never drift down when the full contraction is reached. Maintain a neutral back and neck, especially when approaching MMF.

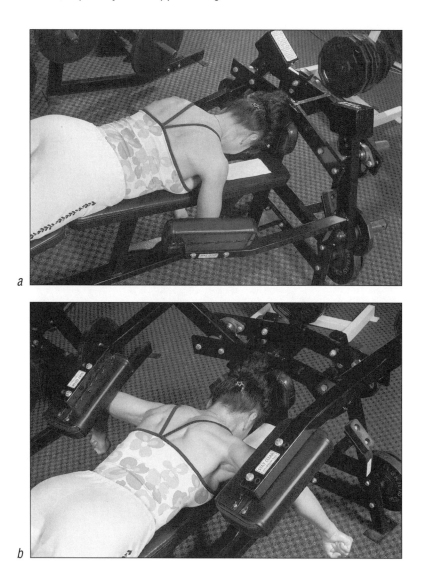

a

b

Dumbbell Iso Post Delt

Primary Movers: posterior deltoids, latissimus dorsi

Type of Movement: single joint, isolation, rotary

Technique

Stand with trunk flexion at 90 degrees, arms extended, and slightly bent elbows perpendicular to the floor. Pull the dumbbells up in a reverse fly movement until the hands are parallel with the ground and pause. Slowly lower the dumbbells to the starting position. Repeat. Maintain a neutral lower back, never allowing hyperextension, and make sure that each rep reaches the same spot at full range of motion.

a

b

Cable Decline Seated Low Row

Primary Movers: latissimus dorsi, posterior deltoids, rhomboids, upper and middle trapezius, biceps

Type of Movement: compound, multijoint, linear

Technique

Sitting backward on a bench with feet flat on the platform and chest against the pad, grasp the handles with the palms perpendicular to the ground. Pull the handles straight back and squeeze with a pause at the full contraction. Then slowly return the handles to the starting position while gently straightening the elbows and keeping tension on the targeted muscles. Repeat. Do not let the wrists flex, especially at the full contraction position. Adduct the scapula to increase rhomboids and trapezius activation.

Cable Iso Decline Post Delt Fly

Primary Movers: latissimus dorsi, post deltoids, rhomboids, upper and middle trapezius

Type of Movement: single joint, isolation, rotary

Technique

Sitting backward on a bench with feet flat on the platform and chest against the pad, grasp the opposing cable handles with a parallel grip and pull back with slightly bent elbows until arms are parallel to the floor and pause. Then slowly return the arms to the starting position, while following a diagonal line. The elbows should be kept in a soft, semilocked position. Repeat.

a

b

Machine Incline High Row Lever

Primary Movers: latissimus dorsi, posterior deltoids, rhomboids, middle and lower trapezius, biceps

Type of Movement: compound, multijoint, linear

Technique

Sitting in the high row machine with the chest firmly pressed against the pad and arms fully extended to reach the handles overhead, grasp the handles with a diagonal grip and pull the lever arms toward the chest while the elbows drive straight back and the wrists stay rigid. Squeeze at the full contraction with a pause and then slowly return the handles to the starting position. Repeat. Keep the chest against the pad at all times and maintain neutral wrists (do not allow flexion).

a   b

Cable Incline Iso High Post Delt

Primary Movers: latissimus dorsi, posterior deltoids, rhomboids, middle and lower trapezius

Type of Movement: single joint, isolation, rotary

Technique

Standing in a stable position with knees slightly bent, grasp the opposing cable handles with a parallel grip and arms on a diagonal incline. Pull the cable handles down on a diagonal until the arms are parallel to the ground and pause. Then slowly lower the weight to the starting position without moving the elbows. Repeat. This can also be performed while sitting on the 90-degree bench.

a

b

Cable Close Grip Lat Pulldown

Primary Movers: latissimus dorsi, posterior deltoids, rhomboids, middle trapezius, biceps

Type of Movement: compound, multijoint, linear

Technique

Sitting on the machine with the thighs secured under the pads, extend the arms straight overhead and grasp the handles with the palms facing each other. Pull the handles down to just above the chest and pause. Make sure that the forearms are always perpendicular to the floor in order to avoid injury to the rotator cuff muscles. Then slowly lower the weight back to the starting position with the arms fully extended, keeping tension on the targeted muscles. Maintain a neutral lower back, never allowing hyperextension, and keep the hips on the seat at all times.

a

b

Cable Wide Grip Lat Pulldown

Primary Movers: latissimus dorsi, posterior deltoids, rhomboids, middle trapezius, biceps

Type of Movement: compound, multijoint, linear

Technique

Sitting on the machine with the thighs secured under the pads, extend the arms straight overhead and grasp the bar slightly wider than shoulder width, with forearms and palms perpendicular to the floor. Pull the handles down to just above the chest and pause. Make sure that the forearms are always perpendicular to the floor to avoid injury to the rotator cuff muscles. Then slowly lower the weight back to the starting position with the arms fully extended, keeping tension on the targeted muscles. Maintain a neutral lower back, never allowing hyperextension, and keep the hips on the seat at all times.

a

b

Body Weight Pull-Up

Primary Movers: latissimus dorsi, posterior deltoids, rhomboids, middle trapezius, biceps

Type of Movement: compound, multijoint, linear

Technique

Grasping the bars with palms perpendicular to the floor and facing one another, pull the body up until the shoulders reach the bars and the hands are just above the chest, then pause. Make sure that the forearms are perpendicular to the floor throughout the entire range of motion. Slowly lower the weight back to the starting position with the arms fully extended, keeping tension on the targeted muscles. Maintain a smooth lift without bouncing on the bottom to initiate movement and without swinging the body. Use weight-assisted pull-up and dip machines to achieve MMF at desired rep ranges. Supination and pronation grips can also be used as long as the forearm stays perpendicular to the floor.

a

b

Machine Iso Lat Pullover (Super Pullover)

Primary Movers: latissimus dorsi, teres major, pectoralis minor

Type of Movement: single joint, isolation, rotary

Technique

Sitting on the machine with the head against the pad and the seat belt tightened firmly, if the machine has one, initiate the pull by driving all the force through the elbows into the pads. Avoid applying pressure to the bar from the forearms or hands, and keep the arms bent at 90 degrees. Pull the pads to the abdomen, 180 degrees, and pause. Then slowly allow the weight to return to the starting position. Repeat. Maintain a neutral back, never allowing it to arch during the movement.

a

b

139

Dumbbell Iso Hammer Curl

Primary Movers: latissimus dorsi, posterior deltoids, rhomboids, upper trapezius, biceps

Type of Movement: compound, multijoint, linear

Technique

Sitting with the back pressed firmly against the 90-degree bench, grasp the dumbbells with palms facing each other and arms extended at the sides. Curl the weight until you reach full flexion. Do not allow elbows to drift forward. Elbow should remain in the positive phase in order to keep the maximum tension on the biceps Then slowly lower the weight while keeping the torso erect and the neck in a neutral position. Repeat.

a

b

Cable Iso Biceps Curls

Primary Movers: biceps brachialis, biceps femoris

Type of Movement: single joint, isolation, rotary

Technique

Standing in a partial diagonal lunge with the rear foot supported against the platform and arms fully extended at the sides, grasp cable handles with the palms in a supine position. Pull up by curling the handles to the full range of motion, with elbow flexion at 130 degrees. Ensure that the upper arms and shoulders remain static throughout the full range of motion. Then slowly lower the handles while keeping the torso and upper arms in a stationary position. Repeat. Two exercise options include the parallel and prone grips.

Dumbbell Iso Biceps Curl

Primary Mover: biceps

Type of Movement: single joint, angular

Technique

Sitting on a 90-degree bench with feet flat on the floor and arms fully extended at the sides, grasp the dumbbells and pull the weight directly up to where the elbows are bent at 130 degrees and pause (full range). Then lower the weight to the starting position, without hyperextending the elbow, and pause again. Repeat. Always maintain a neutral arch in the lower back and a neutral wrist. Do not allow the elbows to drift forward while completing full flexion.

a   b

Bar Wrist Flexion

Primary Movers: wrist flexors (carpi radialis, carpi ulnaris, digitorum superficialis, policis longus)

Type of Movement: single joint, angular

Technique

Place the forearms on the bench with the wrists extended beyond the edge of the bench and palms facing the ceiling. Grasp the barbell with a supinated full grip. Pull the weight up with the wrist flexors, moving the weight toward the forearms, and pause at full contraction. Then slowly lower the weight until it reaches the full range of motion and pause. Repeat.

a

b

Dumbbell Iso-Lateral Wrist Extension

Primary Movers: wrist extensors (carpi radialis, carpi ulnaris)

Type of Movement: single joint, angular

Technique

Place the forearms on the bench with the wrists extended beyond the edge of the bench and palms facing the floor. Grasp the barbell with a pronated full grip. Push the weight up with the wrist extensors, moving the weight toward the top part of the forearms, and pause at full contraction. Then slowly lower the weight until it reaches the full range of motion and pause. Repeat.

a

b

Cable Internal Shoulder Rotation

Primary Movers: subscapularis, pectoralis major

Type of Movement: single joint, isolation, rotary

Technique

Standing in a stable position with knees slightly bent and the arm bent at 90 degrees, with the elbow aligned with the side of the body, grasp the cable handle with the palm perpendicular to the floor. Pull the cable handles across the front of the body to the full range of movement and pause. Then slowly return the weight to the starting position, while keeping the elbow at the side of the body. Repeat. An option for performing this exercise is to sit on a 90-degree bench or to use a Hammer iso lateral internal rotation machine.

a

b

Cable External Shoulder Rotation

Primary Movers: supraspinatus, infraspinatus, teres minor

Type of Movement: single joint, isolation, rotary

Technique

Standing in a stable position with knees slightly bent and the arm bent at 90 degrees, with the elbow aligned with the side of the body, grasp the cable handle with the palm perpendicular to the floor. Push the cable handles out from the body to the full range of movement and pause. Then slowly return the weight to the starting position, while keeping the elbow at the side of the body. Repeat. An option for performing this exercise is to sit on a 90-degree bench or to use a Hammer iso-lateral external rotation machine.

a

b

Dumbbell Iso Shoulder Shrug

Primary Movers: upper traps, upper rhomboids

Type of Movement: single joint, isolation, rotary

Technique

Sitting on 90-degree bench with feet flat on the floor and arms extended down the side of the body, grasp the dumbbells with a full grip and raise the weight while keeping the elbows locked, and pause. Although the shrug is a short range of movement, the rep speed does not change. Focus on the outside of the shoulders elevating toward the ears. Lower the weight to the full range of movement, then pause. Repeat. Always maintain a neutral arch in the lower back and a neutral wrist. Never roll the shoulders, as doing so can increase the risk of trauma to the rotator cuff and acromioclavicular joint.

a

b

Machine Neck Flexion

Primary Mover: sternocleidomastoid

Type of Movement: single joint, isolation, rotary

Technique

Sitting on the neck machine with the face on the pads, and supporting the upper torso so that the shoulders do not move during the movement, push the pads down toward the top of the chest and pause at full range. Then allow the pads to slowly raise to the starting position while keeping tension on the targeted muscles, and pause. Do not hyperextend the neck, and do not bounce at the full contraction. Repeat. Always keep the upper torso erect and maintain good posture.

Machine Neck Extension

Primary Movers: semispinalis, upper traps

Type of Movement: single joint, isolation, rotary

Technique

Sitting on the neck machine with the back of the head on the pads, and supporting the upper torso so that the shoulders do not move during the movement, push the pads down toward the upper back and pause at the full range of motion. Then slowly return the pads to the starting position while keeping tension on the targeted muscles, and pause. Repeat. Always keep the upper torso erect, maintain good posture, and never bounce at the full contraction.

Machine Lateral Neck Left and Right Flexion

Primary Movers: scalenus anticus and posticus, sternocleidomastoid

Type of Movement: single joint, isolation, rotary

Technique

Sitting on the neck machine with the side of the head on the pads and supporting the upper torso so that the shoulders do not move during the movement, push the pads toward the top of the opposite shoulder and pause at full range. Then slowly return the pads to the starting position while keeping tension on the targeted muscles, and pause. Repeat. Maintain good posture, keep the shoulders squared, and never bounce at the full contraction.

Machine Abdominal Crunch

Primary Movers: rectus and transverse abdominis, internal and external obliques

Type of Movement: single joint, isolation, rotary

Technique

Sitting on the abdominal machine with feet flat on the floor if possible and elbows bent at 120 degrees while gently holding the handles above the head, lower the upper torso toward the knees and pause at full range. Throughout the movement, the arms should remain in a static position while the force is driven through the elbows and the abdominals contract. Then slowly lift the torso to the starting position while keeping tension on the targeted muscles, and pause. Blow all the air out of the lungs at the fully contracted position. Repeat.

a

b

LOWER BODY MOVEMENTS: MULTIJOINT AND SINGLE-JOINT

Diagonal Body Weight Lower Back Extension

Primary Movers: erector spinae, gluteus medius

Type of Movement: single joint, isolation, rotary

Technique

Placing the feet on the platform with the heels locked under the lip of the front pad and hips slightly above the pad, bend the waist to 90 degrees and then lift the upper torso until it reaches full extension. Pause. Then slowly lower the torso to the starting position, while keeping tension on the targeted muscles at all times. Repeat. Never hyperextend the lower back beyond neutral posture. The arms can be folded over the chest or a weight can be held over the chest for additional resistance.

a

b

Machine Lower Back Extension

Primary Mover: erector spinae

Type of Movement: single joint, isolation, rotary

Technique

Placing the feet on the platform and securing both seat belts to eliminate lower body involvement and isolate the lower back, grasp the handles while pressing the midback firmly against the pad. Keep the hips firmly against the lower lumbar pad. Push the upper torso back until it reaches full extension to neutral posture (90 degrees) and pause. Then slowly lower the torso to the starting position (approximately 60 degrees) while keeping tension on the targeted muscles at all times. Repeat. Never hyperextend the lower back beyond the 90 degrees.

a

b

Smith Machine Stiff-Leg Deadlift

Primary Movers: erector spinae, gluteus medius and minimus

Type of Movement: single joint, isolation, rotary

Technique

Placing the feet shoulder-width apart on the platform with the torso bent to 90 degrees, knees slightly bent, and arms extended down, grasp the bar with a pronated grip, or with an under- and overgrip for heavier weight. Extend the upper torso up until it is just shy of neutral posture, or at full extension, and pause. Then slowly lower the torso to the starting position while keeping tension on the targeted muscles at all times. Repeat. Never hyperextend the lower back beyond a neutral position.

a

b

Machine Seated Leg Press

Primary Movers: gluteus maximus and minimus, quads, hamstrings

Type of Movement: compound, multijoint, linear

Technique

Sitting on the leg press machine with feet flat on the platform, shoulder-width apart, and the hips and knees bent to approximately 90 degrees, grasp the handles with a light grip and press the platform away from the body, primarily using the heels of the feet, until the legs are extended to just shy of full extension. Pause. Never place the majority of resistance on the balls of the feet and toes. Then slowly lower the platform toward the body, making sure the weight does not bounce off the weight stack during the transition. Pause. Repeat. Keep the knees in line with the shoulders and hips at all times and maintain a neutral neck position throughout the entire movement.

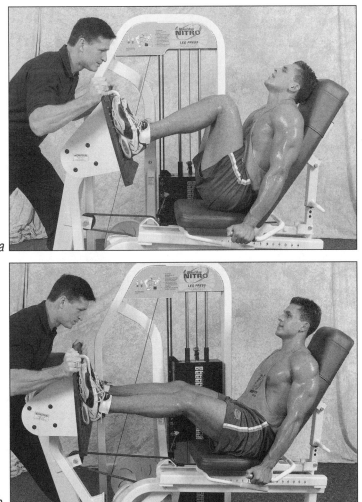

a

b

Machine Sissy Squat

Primary Movers: gluteus maximus and minimus, quads, hamstrings

Type of Movement: compound, multijoint, linear

Technique

Placing the feet shoulder-width apart behind the pads and flat on the platform, slowly lower the body until the quads are parallel with the floor and pause. The back should bend approximately 15 to 20 degrees over the quads. Then slowly extend the body up until the back is perpendicular to the floor and there is a slight bend at the hips. Repeat, keeping the knees in line with the shoulders and hips at all times. The arms can be crossed in front of the chest, or a weight can be held for added resistance.

a

b

Smith Machine Deadlift

Primary Movers: erector spinae, gluteus medius and minimus, quads, hamstrings

Type of Movement: compound, multijoint, linear

Technique

Placing the feet shoulder-width apart on the platform with the arms extended down and palms in a pronated or under- and overgrip, squat to a 90-degree knee flexion and bend forward at the hips to approximately 45 degrees. Pull the weight up until the torso reaches full extension while maintaining a slight bend in the hips and knees. Pause. Then slowly lower the weight to the starting position while keeping tension on the targeted muscles. Repeat. Never hyperextend the lower back during the full extension.

a

b

Dumbbell Lunge

Primary Movers: gluteus maximus and minimus, quads, hamstrings

Type of Movement: compound, multijoint, linear

Technique

Stand in a straddle position with one foot touching the wall and the other foot extended backward, with the feet shoulder-width apart and the arms extended down, holding the dumbbells with a full grip. Slowly lower the torso until the back knee is right above the floor and the front quad is parallel to the floor. Pause. Then slowly raise the torso to the starting position, stopping just shy of the front knee locking, and pause. Repeat. Keep the knees in line with the shoulders and hips at all times, and never allow the front knee to drift over the toes, or the rear knee or foot to drift internally or externally. Performing the single-leg repeat against the wall controls the lunge angle and facilitates MMF, whereas walking lunges do not maintain constant muscle tension.

a

b

Hip Extension

Primary Movers: erector spinae, gluteus medius and minimus

Type of Movement: single joint, isolation, rotary

Technique

Bending over the hip extensor machine, extend the arms to grab the machine in order to stabilize the body. Push the hips and legs to a full hip extension and pause. Then slowly lower the hip and leg to the starting position while keeping tension on the targeted muscles. Repeat. Never hyperextend the lower back during the concentric movement. For variety and maximum hip extensor hypertrophy and strength, use a Nautilus duo hip extension machine.

a

b

Primary Movers: sartorius, gracilis, iliopsoas

Type of Movement: single joint, isolation, rotary

Technique

Keep the elbows on the machine pads to support the body in an erect position, with the hips slightly flexed and the back flat against the pad. Pull the knees up toward the chest while keeping the shins perpendicular to the floor. Pause. Then slowly lower the legs to the starting position while maintaining a flat back, keeping tension on the targeted muscles the entire time. Pause. Never allow the chest to bend forward or the feet to extend forward.

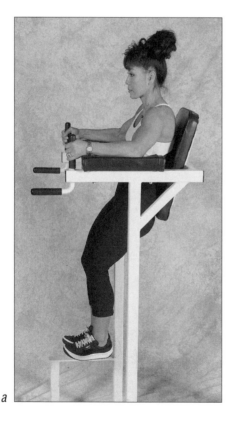

a

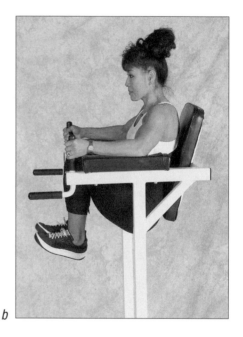

b

Machine Hip Flexion

Primary Movers: sartorius, gracilis, iliopsoas

Type of Movement: single joint, isolation, rotary

Technique

Supporting the body in an erect position with the machine handles and keeping the hips slightly flexed, pull the knee up toward the chest while keeping the shin perpendicular to the floor. Pause. Then slowly lower the leg to the starting position while keeping tension on the targeted muscles and pause. Repeat. Never allow the chest to bend forward or the knee or foot to extend forward.

a

b

Machine Hip Abduction

Primary Movers: gluteus medius, tensor fascia latae

Type of Movement: single joint, isolation, rotary

Technique

Sitting with the back pressed against the pad and the hands on the machine handles to stabilize the torso in an erect position, while the outer thighs and knees contact the pads at 90 degrees' flexion, push the knees away from the midline of the body to the full range of motion and pause. Then slowly bring the knees back to the starting position while keeping tension on the targeted muscles, and pause. Repeat. For variety, allow the torso to bend forward to an erect position. This will target the gluteus medius.

a

b

Machine Hip Adduction

Primary Movers: adductors longus, magnus, and brevis

Type of Movement: single joint, isolation, rotary

Technique

Sitting with the hands on the machine handles to stabilize the torso in an erect position, while the outer thighs and knees contact the pads at 90 degrees' flexion, pull the knees toward the midline of the body to the full range of motion and pause, pads touching. Then slowly bring the knees back to the starting position while keeping tension on the targeted muscles and pause. Repeat.

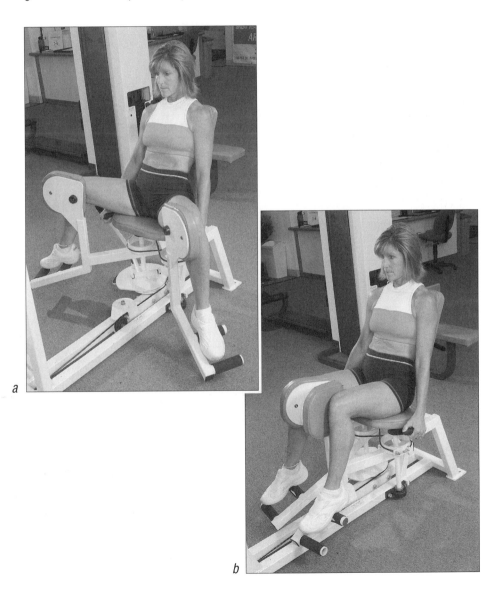

a

b

Machine Leg Extension

Primary Movers: biceps femoris, semitendinosus, semimembranosus

Type of Movement: single joint, isolation, rotary

Technique

Starting in a seated position with the hands on the machine handles to stabilize the torso against the pad, knees flexed at 90 degrees, and pads placed just above the feet in dorsiflexion, push the feet up to reach full extension with the legs parallel to the floor, and pause. Then slowly lower the feet to the starting position while keeping tension on the targeted muscles, and pause. Repeat.

a

b

Machine Leg Curl (Flexion)

Primary Movers: biceps femoris, semitendinosus, semimembranosus

Type of Movement: single joint, isolation, rotary

Technique

Lying in a prone position on an angular bench with the hands grasping the handles for trunk stability, kneecaps placed slightly over the edge of the bench, and the resistance pads resting just above the heels, pull the ankles up toward the gluteus maximus to the full range of motion and pause. Then slowly lower the ankles to the starting position while keeping tension on the targeted muscles, and pause. Repeat. The ankles are held in neutral dorsiflexion, and the hips remain in contact with the bench throughout the entire range of motion. Never allow the knees, back, or neck to hyperextend. For variety, add controlled hip extension at the end of the concentric movement, while in complete flexion, for additional hip extension and lower back activation.

a

b

Seated Machine Leg Curl (Flexion)

Primary Movers: biceps femoris, semitendinosus, semimembranosus

Type of Movement: single joint, isolation, rotary

Technique

Sitting on the machine with the kneecaps placed slightly forward of the thigh stability pads and the ankles against the resistance pads, push the ankles toward the gluteus maximus to the full range of motion and pause. Then slowly return the ankles to the starting position while keeping tension on the targeted muscles and pause. Repeat. Throughout the movement, the hands should grasp the handles for trunk stability and the ankles should be held in neutral dorsiflexion while the hips and lower back remain in contact with the bench. Never allow the knees or back to hyperextend. For variety, use the standing isolateral leg curl for varied hamstring stimulation.

a

b

Machine Gastrocnemius Raise

Primary Mover: gastrocnemius

Type of Movement: single joint, isolation, rotary

Technique

Bending over the machine with the legs fully extended and the balls and toes of the feet on the platform in dorsiflexion, push the pad on the lower back until the ankles are in full plantar flexion and pause. Then slowly lower the platform to the starting position, keeping tension on the targeted muscles the entire time, and pause. Repeat. Never bounce at the end of the eccentric contraction. Reduce the weight if the full range of motion cannot be maintained throughout the entire set.

a

b

Machine Soleus Raise

Primary Mover: soleus

Type of Movement: single joint, isolation, rotary

Technique

Sitting with the resistance pad directly over the lower part of the quad, just above the knee, and legs flexed at 90 degrees with the balls of the feet and toes on the platform in dorsiflexion, push the pad up until the ankles reach full plantar flexion and pause. Then slowly lower the pad to the starting position, keeping tension on the targeted muscles, and pause. Repeat. Never bounce at the end of the eccentric contraction. Reduce the weight if the full range of motion cannot be maintained throughout the entire set.

a

b

Manual Shin Curl

Primary Mover: tibialis anterior

Type of Movement: single joint, isolation, rotary

Technique

Sit on a flat bench with one leg fully extended and the lower part of the leg held partially over the edge of the bench, with the foot in full plantar flexion, and the opposite leg bent with the foot flat on the floor for stabilization. Pull the ankle and foot up toward the knee to achieve dorsiflexion, keeping the leg straight and minimizing quad recruitment. Then slowly lower the ankle and foot to the starting position, keeping tension on the targeted muscles, and pause. Repeat. Placing resistance over the big toe, instead of over the top of the ankle, isolates the extensor hallucis longus instead of the tibialis anterior. An option for this exercise is to use the Hammer shin curl machine.

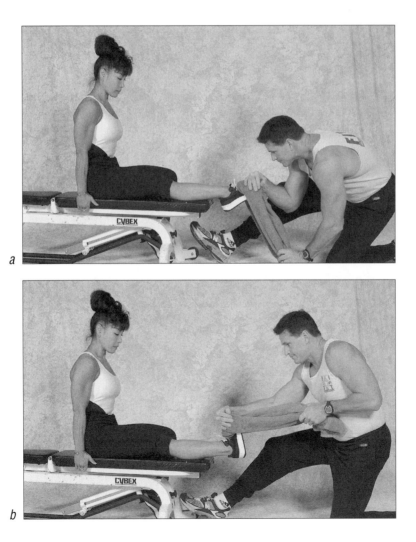

a

b

Manual Resistance Exercises

The HIT strength system uses manual resistance exercises, or manuals, as a way to create variety and add additional AOT to the strength program. Manual strength training is the single greatest tool that athletes and coaches can have in their strength training toolbox. NSPA's success with traditional weightlifters integrating manuals into their routines has been phenomenal; their usual comments are "I've never felt such a pump," "I'm really feeling all my muscles work," "I can't believe how intense this set was," and "I've been lifting for 10 years but never felt this level of muscle burn."

Manual strength training involves two people working together to perform an exercise without relying on weights or machines. This technique teaches athletes how to apply resistance to movement, both positive and negative, and encourages smooth, fluid motion through the entire strength curve of the exercise. Through the use of manuals, athletes can also refine spotting skills, learn which muscles contract to perform movement, and become familiar with the biomechanics and strength curve associated with each movement

I have been using manuals for more than 25 years and believe that this technique is the most important tool an athlete can master. I guarantee that once athletes have learned how to perform manuals properly, their knowledge of muscles, proper lifting techniques, and spotting will be enhanced greatly.

NSPA has taught thousands of trainers and athletes how to perform manuals. The best way to learn this technique is to work with someone who is a HIT specialist; otherwise, bad habits can be formed very quickly. Athletes must understand that manual techniques are difficult and demand a great deal of concentration to perfect. And, most important, athletes need to be aware that, if done incorrectly, manuals can cause injury.

To correctly perform manual strength training, the spotter applies positive resistance similar to any free weight or machine while the lifter exerts 100 percent effort, pushing against the spotter's resistance. The positive movement must be completed in three to four seconds and is accompanied by a distinct pause at full range of motion. During the pause, the spotter continues to apply resistance and never allows the muscle to relax. This is then followed by the stronger, negative phase of the movement, where the spotter must apply even greater resistance—20 to 40 percent more than during the positive phase. During the negative phase, the lifter must be prepared to exert 100 percent effort while trying to resist the spotter. There is no machine on the market today that can apply this type of strength resistance to a given strength curve of an exercise, which makes manuals unique.

There are some disadvantages to using manual resistance training, and anyone learning the technique should also be aware of these limitations. For example, there must be two people to make it work, and both need to be proficient with the technique. Also, if one person is significantly stronger than the other, it could be difficult for the weaker person to bring the stronger person to MMF, although this can be managed through appropriate use of levers and preexhaustion iso-lateral movements. Probably the most significant limitation is that manuals do not have measurable strength accountability, for instance, pressing 60 pounds for 10 reps in 60 seconds.

There are also many advantages to using manual resistance, and, in my opinion, these far outweigh the limitations. For example, no equipment is needed, so manuals can be performed anywhere, in any setting. When large groups of athletes need to train at the same time, they can easily train to 100 percent MMF by pairing up and assisting each other with manual resistance. Manuals can be used in conjunction with weights and machines to overcome a sticking point and provide enhanced AOT.

The following guidelines are important to follow when performing manuals:

▶ The trainer should maintain even pressure through the full range of motion during both the positive and negative phases and should increase the manual resistance during the negative phase to accommodate the 20 to 40 percent inherent increase in strength during the eccentric component of the lift.

▶ The athlete and trainer must be in constant communication to achieve maximum results within the set rep range to MMF.

▶ The goal for the athlete is to push maximally for every rep. The trainer is completely in control of the resistance and speed of movement to maximize muscle fiber recruitment.

▶ The trainer must learn how to use body weight, levers, and devices such as ropes, handles, towels, stability balls and so on to apply the appropriate amount of resistance and to become mechanically efficient.

▶ The neck, shoulders, back, and wrists must be kept neutral for every lift.

Prone Decline Push-Up (M)

The athlete starts in a lowered position one inch from the ground. The trainer applies manual resistance to the upper back and shoulder area at the beginning of the push and throughout the entire lift. A neutral back and neck should be maintained. Place one leg on a stability ball during the push-up for advanced core challenge.

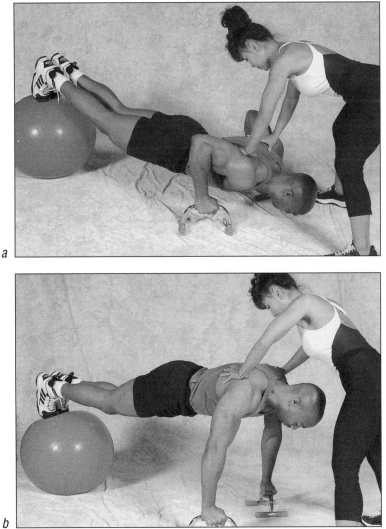

a

b

Seated Chest Press (M)

The athlete starts with the arms flexed at the elbows. The trainer applies manual resistance to the decline horizontal chest press through increased strap pressure at the beginning of the push and throughout the entire lift. The trainer's body weight can be used to stabilize the resistance.

a

b

Iso Straight Arm Chest Cross (S)

The athlete starts with the arm extended straight out to the side. The trainer applies manual resistance to the wrist (or to the elbow for increased leverage) at the beginning of the push and throughout the entire lift as the arm moves across the chest.

a

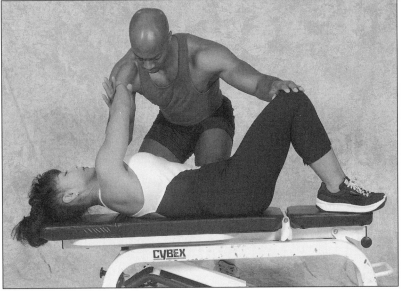

b

Seated High Row:
Post Delt Emphasis (M)

The athlete starts with the arms extended to the front and maintains a slight horizontal incline angle at the start of the pull and throughout the entire lift. The trainer applies manual resistance to the straps. When the palms are held parallel to each other and the elbows are kept close to the side, the lats are emphasized. Palms held horizontally to the floor emphasize the upper traps and posterior delts. A stability ball can be used to assist with leverage.

a

b

Seated Low Row, Close Grip: Lat Emphasis (M)

The athlete starts with the arms extended to the front and maintains a slight horizontal decline angle with the palms parallel at the beginning of the pull and throughout the entire lift. The trainer applies manual resistance to the straps while placing the feet on the bench to add extra leverage.

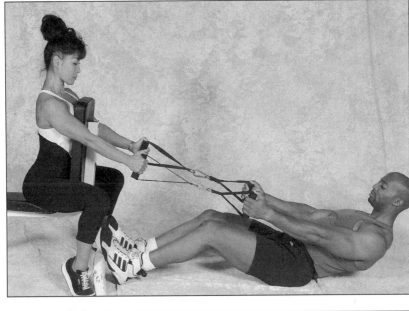

a

b

Seated Iso Horizontal Row With Post Delt Emphasis (M)

The athlete starts in a sitting position with chest firmly against the pad. Extend one arm horizontally in front while the trainer applies resistance to the forearm or wrist through the full range of motion.

a

b

Iso Post Delt (S)

The athlete positions the body in a three-point kneeling position while the trainer applies resistance at the elbow for increased muscle isolation. The trainer must use body weight and body levers to assist with the resistance. This exercise can also be done with the elbow to the side, simulating a super pull-over with emphasis on the lats.

a

b

Iso Prone Post Delt (S)

The athlete lies on a bench in a prone position with the hands behind the head. The trainer applies resistance on the elbows through the full range of motion as the athlete raises the elbows to be parallel to the floor.

a

b

Seated Iso Shoulder Press (M)

The athlete sits with the elbows flexed to 180 degrees at the side of the body, palms facing forward, and hands closed with rigid wrists. The trainer applies manual resistance to the tops of the fists at the beginning of the push and throughout the entire lift. For variety, internally rotate the palms or adduct the elbows up to 90 degrees to emphasize anterior deltoid recruitment.

a

b

Inverted Seated Shoulder Press (M)

The athlete starts in an inverted trunk position with the feet on a stability ball, trunk flexed to 90 degrees, arms bent, and hands parallel at the beginning of the push. The torso is then pressed straight up by the push-up handles. For variety, remove one leg from the ball and extend overhead to increase the resistance and the core stabilization challenge.

a

b

Seated Iso Lateral Raise (S)

The athlete sits with arms to the side, elbows flexed to 90 degrees, and palms open. The trainer applies manual resistance to the elbows at the beginning of the push and throughout the entire lift.

a

b

Supine Iso Frontal Raise (S)

The athlete lies in a prone position on a bench with the arms extended vertically and palms open. The trainer applies manual resistance to the wrist at the beginning of the push and throughout the entire lift.

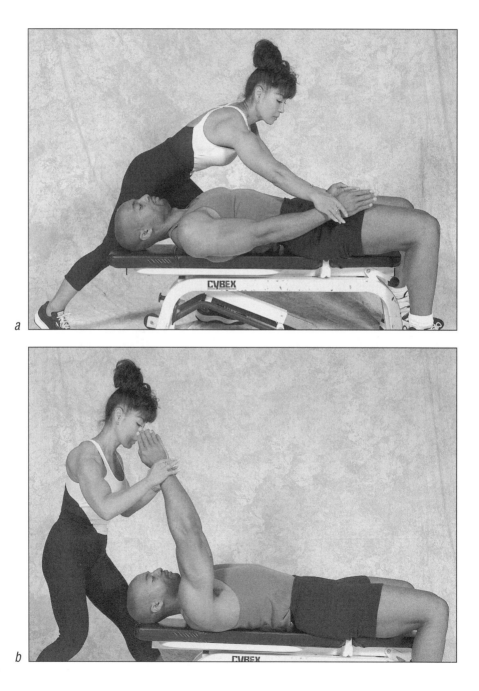

a

b

Supine Decline Lat Pulldown (M)

The athlete lies in a supine position on a decline bench with the arms extended straight overhead and palms in a supinated position. The trainer applies manual resistance to the straps at the beginning of the pull and throughout the entire lift.

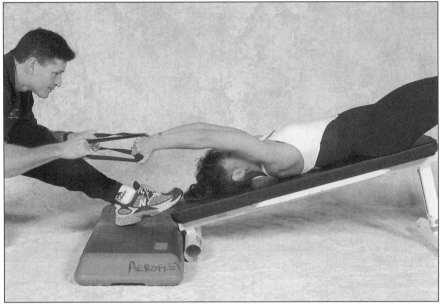

a

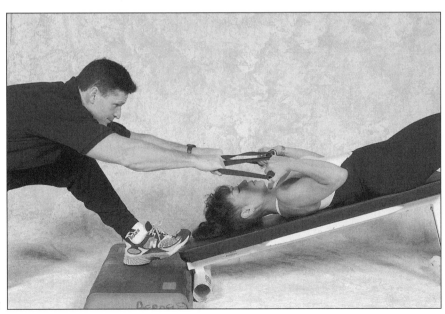

b

Supine Iso Lat Pulldown (S)

The athlete lies in a supine position on a decine bench with the arms bent at 90° and palms open and parallel to each other. The trainer applies manual resistance (pulling) behind the elbows throughout the entire range of motion.

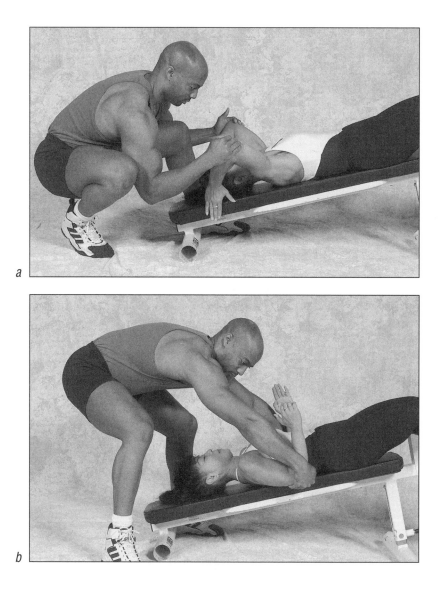

a

b

Supine Iso Biceps Curl (S)

The athlete lies in a supine position on a mat with the arms extended horizontally to the side and palms grasping the resistance straps. The trainer applies manual resistance to the straps at the beginning of the pull and throughout the entire lift.

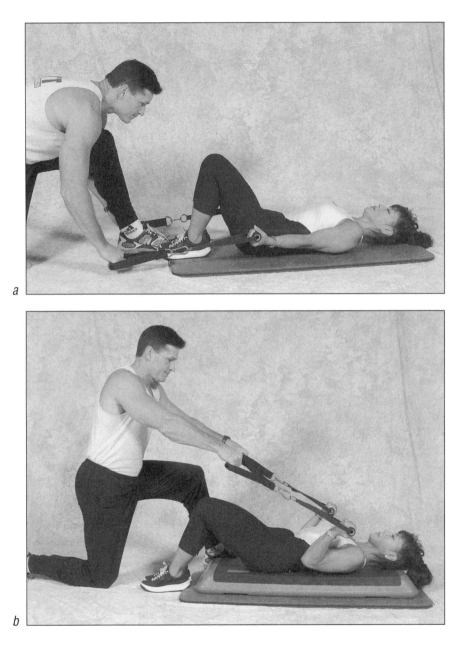

a

b

Supine Iso Triceps Extension (S)

The athlete lies in a supine position on a mat with the elbows lifted and flexed to 130 degrees and the palms open and parallel to each other. The trainer applies manual resistance behind the wrists at the beginning of the push and throughout the entire lift.

a

b

Seated Triceps Extension (S)

The athlete sits with the arms extended overhead, elbows flexed to 130 degrees, and palms grasping the resistance straps. The trainer applies manual resistance to the straps at the beginning of the push and throughout the entire lift.

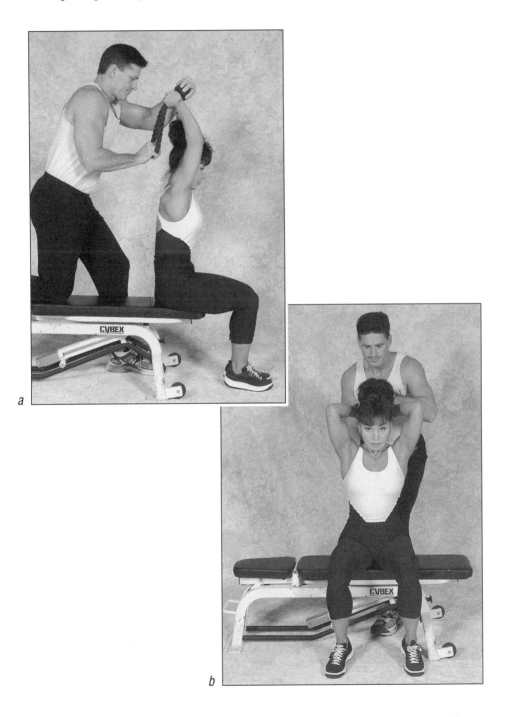

a

b

Prone Stability Ball Triceps Extension (S)

The athlete starts in a prone position in a full body extension with the arms under the chest, elbows flexed to 130 degrees, and palms open and grasping the ball. Manual resistance can be applied to the shoulders during the lift if greater resistance is desired.

a

b

Supine Neck Flexion (S)

The athlete starts in a supine bench position with the hands positioned on the hips. The trainer applies manual resistance to the forehead and jaw at the beginning of the pull and throughout the entire lift.

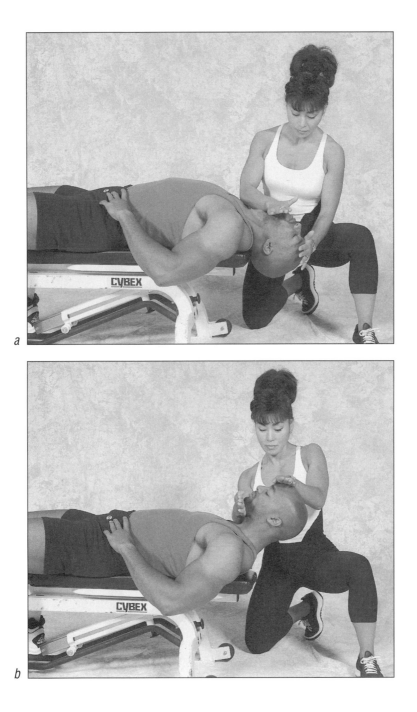

a

b

Prone Neck Extension (S)

The athlete starts in a prone bench position with elbows flexed at the side of the body and hands providing stabilization by holding onto the bench. The trainer applies manual resistance to the back of the head at the beginning of the push and throughout the entire lift.

a

b

Seated Neck Lateral Flexion (S)

The athlete sits with the arms at the side of the body and hands on the thighs for stabilization. The trainer applies manual resistance to the right side of the head at the beginning of the pull and throughout the entire lift. Repeat for the left side of the neck.

a

b

Supine Stability Ball Crunch (S)

The athlete starts in a supine position with the midback and hips on the stability ball, hands behind the head or neck, and upper arms parallel to the floor and relaxed. The athlete then lifts the trunk upward at the beginning of the pull. For additional resistance, the trainer may apply manual resistance to the elbows at the beginning of the pull and throughout the entire lift.

Supine Leg Cross
Opposite-Elbow-to-Knee Crunch (S)

The athlete lies in a supine position on a mat with the left elbow flexed, hand behind the head, upper arm parallel to the floor and relaxed, and right leg crossed at the knee. The athlete pulls the trunk diagonally upward at the beginning of the pull and throughout the entire lift. Repeat for the right side. For additional resistance, the trainer may apply manual resistance to the elbow at the beginning of the pull and throughout the entire lift.

a

b

Supine Crossover Crunch (S)

The athlete lies in a supine position on a mat with the right elbow flexed, hand behind the head, upper arm parallel to the floor and relaxed, and legs parallel to each other and flexed at the knees. The trainer applies resistance at the elbow while stabilizing the athlete at the knee. The athlete rotates the trunk upward and over at the beginning of the pull. Repeat for the left side.

a

b

Supine Pure Abs (S)

The athlete lies in a supine position on a mat with both arms extended and hands open. The athlete lifts the trunk upward at the beginning of the pull to approximately 30 degrees flexion. For additional resistance, the trainer may apply manual resistance to the shoulders at the beginning of the pull and throughout the entire lift.

a

b

Supine Upper Abs (S)

The athlete lies in a supine position on a mat, hands behind the head. The trainer applies resistance to the elbows at the beginning of trunk flexion and throughout the entire lift. Elbows can be positioned close or wide.

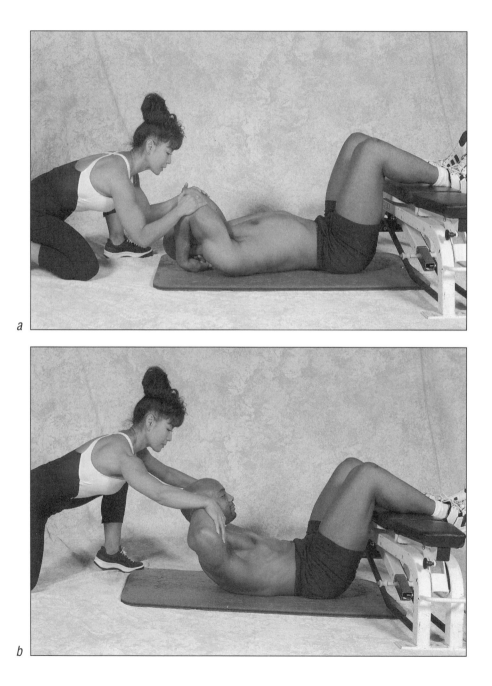

a

b

Supine Oblique Crunch (S)

The athlete lies in a supine position on a mat with the left hand behind the head, right hand on the left hip for stabilization, legs parallel to each other, and knees flexed to 45 degrees. The trainer applies resistance to the left elbow at the beginning of the trunk diagonal flexion and throughout the entire lift.

a

b

Prone Stability Ball Core Abs (S)

The athlete starts in a prone push-up position with feet plantar flexed on the ball and then pulls the lower body into a pike position, or 90 degrees trunk flexion. For additional resistance, the trainer may apply manual resistance to the hips at the beginning of the pull and throughout the entire lift.

a

b

Supine Hip Flexor and Lower Abs (S)

The athlete starts in a supine position on a mat with both arms extended and grasping the trainer's ankles for stability. The trainer applies resistance to the knees at the beginning of the hip flexion and throughout the entire lift. Do not roll the lower back if the athlete has a history of back problems

a

b

Prone Stability Ball Decline Hip and Lower Back Extension (S)

The athlete starts in a prone position on a stability ball with the hips and abs contacting the ball, both elbows flexed to 120 degrees, and hands on the floor stabilizing the body in a pike position over the ball. The athlete pushes the lower back and hip into a vertical extension at the beginning of the extension and throughout the entire lift. For additional resistance, the trainer may apply manual resistance to the heel or ankle at the beginning of the pull and throughout the entire lift.

a

b

Prone Stability Ball
Lower Back Extension (S)

The athlete starts in a prone position on a stability ball with hips and abs in contact, both arms bent 120 degrees, hands across the chest. The trainer applies stabilizing resistance to the ankles. The athlete extends the lower back vertically to perform the lift. For additional resistance, the trainer can lock the heels or apply manuals to the upper back through the lift.

a

b

Prone Stability Ball Decline Iso Hip Extension (S)

The athlete starts in a prone position on a stability ball with the hips and abs contacting the ball, both elbows flexed to 120 degrees, and hands on the floor for stabilization. The trainer applies resistance to the heels and stabilizes the lower back at the beginning of the iso hip extension and throughout the entire lift.

a

b

Supine Bench Iso Hip Flexion (S)

The athlete starts in a supine position on the bench with both arms extended and hands grasping the bench for stabilization. The trainer applies manual resistance to the left knee at the beginning of the pull and throughout the entire lift. Repeat with the right leg and knee.

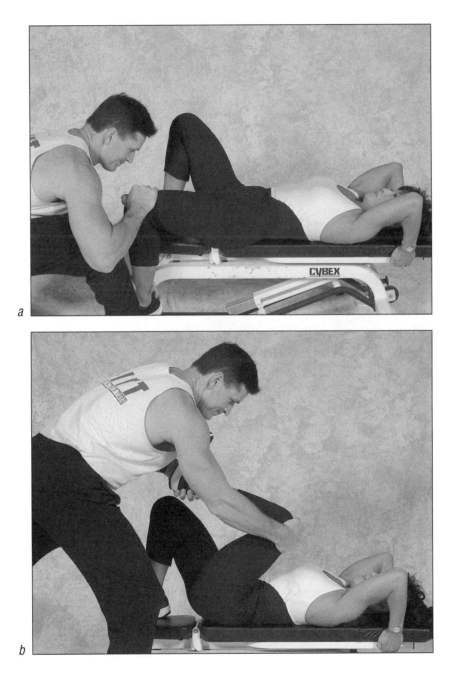

a

b

Body Weight Hip and Quad Extension (Sissy Squat) (M)

The athlete stands in a vertical position with arms extended in front of the body, parallel to the floor, palms open. The trainer applies manual support to the back of the knees and can use increased back extension body weight for greater stability as necessary. The athlete lowers the body in a slow, controlled movement; pauses at the bottom; and then transitions to the push of the lift. For additional resistance, the trainer may apply manual resistance to the shoulders at the beginning of the push and throughout the entire lift. (This will require the trainer to secure his or her lower leg and foot.)

a

b

Prone Stability Ball Hamstring Curl (S)

The athlete lies in a prone position on a stability ball with the hips and abdominals contacting the ball, elbows flexed to 120 degrees, and hands on the floor to stabilize the body position over the ball. The trainer applies manual resistance to the heels at the beginning of the pull and throughout the entire lift. This exercise may also be done one leg at a time.

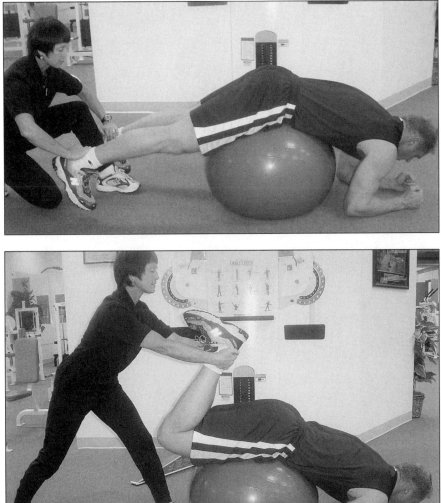

a

b

Iso Hip Abductor (S)

The athlete lies on a mat on the left side with the left knee flexed to 90 degrees, right leg straight, right elbow flexed to 90 degrees, and hand placed on the floor for stabilization. The trainer applies manual resistance to the right knee while stabilizing the hip with the knee or quad at the athlete's lower back and hand on hip at the beginning of the push and throughout the entire lift. Repeat with the opposite leg.

a

b

Iso Hip Adductor (S)

The athlete lies on a mat on the right side with the right knee flexed to 90 degrees, left leg straight, left elbow flexed to 90 degrees, and hand placed on the floor for stabilization. The trainer applies manual resistance with a towel to the left knee and lower leg while stabilizing the athlete's hip with the lower leg and foot at the beginning of the pull and throughout the entire lift. Repeat with the opposite leg.

a

b

Standing Iso Lunge (M)

The athlete starts in a standing vertical position with the arms extended at the side of the body, elbows flexed to 45 degrees, and palms open. The trainer applies manual resistance to the shoulders at the starting position of the lunge and throughout the entire lift. The athlete maintains an erect torso with the feet hip-width apart as the left leg leads into the lunge. The left lower leg remains perpendicular to the floor with the knee over the heel. The knee must never be allowed to travel over the toe. Repeat with the right leg.

a

b

Standing Iso Toe Raise (S)

The athlete stands in a vertical position with the arms extended to the sides, elbows flexed to 45 degrees, and palms open. The trainer applies manual resistance to the shoulders at the beginning of the push and throughout the entire lift. The athlete maintains an erect torso with the left leg straight and the foot on a step. The right lower knee remains flexed. Repeat with the right leg.

a

b

Seated Iso Shin Curl (S)

The athlete sits on a bench with the right leg extended and the midcalf supported on the bench. The ankle is plantar flexed. The trainer applies manual resistance to the top of the foot at the beginning of the pull and throughout the entire lift. During the movement, the athlete should focus on minimizing quad contraction. Repeat with the left foot.

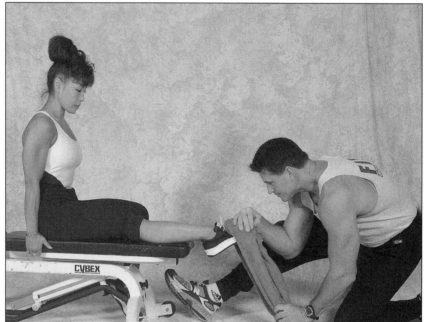

a

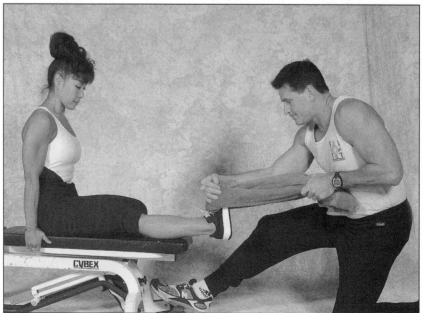

b

About the Author

John C. Philbin is the founder and president of the National Strength Professionals Association (NSPA), a nationally recognized strength and conditioning and personal training certification organization. He has 25 years of experience working with athletes at all levels. He was a strength coach for the Washington Redskins football organization under the legendary Dan Riley for eight years and was the Olympic head coach and director of sports science and conditioning for the U.S. bobsled team from 1988 to 1992. Additionally, Philbin was director of strength and conditioning for the U.S. Olympic Training Center in Lake Placid, New York, and was the conditioning coach for Fernando Vargas, WBA world junior middleweight boxing champion.

Philbin was on the U.S. national bobsled team in 1984 and was an All-American decathlete. He has written four training manuals used in courses taught through NSPA, and he teaches on a regular basis with Dr. Wayne Westcott, fitness research director at the South Shore YMCA in Quincy, Massachusetts.

Philbin lives in Damascus, Maryland.